20 TRILLION FOR HEIRS

How Much for the Lord?

THE FINAL TITHE

A Christian Approach to Estate Planning

By
Rollyn H. Samp, J.D.

Rushmore House Publishing, Sioux Falls, South Dakota 57101 • 800-456-1895

ISBN 0-9624593-7-2
Library of Congress
Catalog Card Number: 99-085842

Second Edition

Edited by: Karen A. Samp, Kristi Franklin and Margaret Mesmer

Illustrations and graphic design: Richard Gorsuch and Neil Isaacson
Special Assistant to Author: Rebecca Vostad
Printed in the United States of America

DISCLAIMER

Portions of this book utilize tax code provisions which reflect the law at the time of publication. Readers should not rely on these references in their own planning as they are for illustration and educational purposes only. Tax laws, regulations and interpretations frequently change.

Likewise, none of the legal forms or clauses should be used in personal estate plans as the meaning and validity can vary from state to state.

All estate planning should be done with the assistance of a professional who can provide the appropriate tax and legal interpretations for individual estate planning.

Congress is currently considering major tax changes that could affect the examples illustrated in this book.

DEDICATION

To my great-grandparents, the Burmasters, Zanggers, Habegers, Klostreichs, and Samps who had the courage to seek religious freedom in America.

To my grandparents, Albert and Vada Samp, Jake and Rosella Habeger whose faith was a daily part of their lives.

To my parents, Elden and Ardyce Samp who were tithers and givers as a living witness.

To my father- and mother-in-law, Jack and Sally Moore who gave of themselves and their tithes for their deep beliefs.

To my aunts and uncles — few have been blessed with such an extended family who supported me at critical times in my life — Ralph and LaVonne Hass, Dr. Jerry and Eileen Marek, and Thomas and Joycelyn Patton.

To my wife, Karen whose prayer, patience, partnership, parenting and professionalism have inspired me each day of our marriage.

To my children and their spouses, Michael and Julie Samp, Rebecca Vostad, Matthew Samp and Elizabeth Samp who are the blessings of life. Each has inspired me.

To my grandchildren, Jacob and Maggie Samp; and future grandchildren who are challenged to carry on a family tradition of serving and giving.

To my entire staff who has accommodated a major book project in the middle of their challenging schedules and have all contributed to this work.

To a special group of pastors who have positively impacted my life at critical times:

Rev. Richard N. and Deloris Nelson
Rev. Norval and Marilyn Wigtil
Pastor A. Richard (Pete) Petersen
Pastor Darrel and Mary Pterson
Pastor Luther and Laurie Anderson
Pastor Noel and Sharon Vold
Pastor Jerry and Paula Merkouris
Rev. Dr. Rol Kindem
Rev. Ed Bersagel

And to a special group who have many talents, but among them the gift of encouragement:

Richard Gorsuch, his wife Bonny, Colour and Sketch who sacrificed family time to complete a graphical work which communicates the words.
Neil Isaacson and his family who made similar sacrifices.
Rev. John and Ruth Lundin
Raul and Roz Ridgeway
Rev. Dr. Al and Alida VerBurg

And each person who reviewed the manuscripts through six editings to complete this work.

BY ROLLYN H. SAMP, J.D.

Celebrate the joy of giving

Prevent family fights over your estate

Have your OWN Will – not the government's

Make stewardship part of your estate plan

Improve family communication concerning giving

Minimize government taxation of your property

Prevent courts from selecting a guardian for your children

Know basic estate-planning tools

Consider organ donation as a gift

And be remembered forever

The Final Tithe:

A Christian Approach to Estate Planning

CONTENTS

F O R E W O R D

the Joy of Giving!

by Dr. George K. Brushaber

President, Bethel College and Seminary
Chm. Senior Editors "Christianity Today"

Not far from my house is a Scandinavian bakery which, from the outside, looks quite unremarkable.

Without stepping over the transom you might deduce that, as a business, good things are accomplished by its presence in the community. Revenue is generated. People are employed.

But early in the morning, push open the door with the tinkling bell, and you realize that behind the door is something more than an economic reality.

A riotous cacophony of sights and smells bombards your senses. On neat shelves against the bleached pine paneling sit row upon row of mouth-watering creations. Asiago cheese rolls crowned with caramelized onion. Finnish apple munnkki, Swedish limpa.

You pause for a moment to breathe deeply the tantalizing aroma of bread warm from the oven. A cook with a broad smile and sparkling eyes, drying her hands on a starched white apron, motions you to a table of generous samples. "You must try this one. I think you will not be able to resist."

In similar ways, from the outside, most would agree that estate planning is a good thing to do. Wealth is transferred in an orderly fashion. Families are protected. Taxes are avoided. Gifting intentions are respected. But there's more.

Push open the door and see God's abundance. Breathe the intoxicating fragrance of His love. Sample the joy of giving – and you'll find in Rollyn Samp's wise counsel ways to satisfy your appetite for more.

May I add a personal word?

Darleen and I know the joy of giving firsthand. We have pushed open the door, crossed over the threshold, and we are savoring the delights of giving. This includes our current giving, but we have also committed ourselves to "The Final Tithe" you will read about in this remarkable volume.

We are experiencing the joy of giving resources to our children and exhilarating joy of giving to the ministries that most stir our hearts and passions. The Epicurean pleasures of fresh baked pastries, wonderful though they are, alas are fleeting (but fattening of course!). The joy of investing in the Lord's work and in the lives of His people gives us lasting satisfaction and pleasure.

But I have also seen firsthand the joy of giving captivate and infuse the lives of others. For many years it has been my good fortune to be invited into the lives of generous women and men who have the *gift of giving*. These friends have relished and reveled in the pure joy of giving. What a zest for life they have!

My grandfather was a German master baker. Although more than half a century has passed, I still remember vividly how irresistible were the aromas and tempting tastes of his beautiful creations just taken from the oven. His shop was the neighborhood gathering place, a magnet where people were drawn and where they lingered enraptured. Just so, people who exude the joy of giving have such an attraction for the rest of us. We are irresistibly drawn to them, not by the gifts we hope to receive, but by the pure appeal of their lives. Theirs are grace-filled lives, full of wisdom and good decisions, but free from guile or the desire to manipulate and gain advantage. Just to know people who have found the joy of giving is sufficient to be blessed oneself.

The blessings their lives bestow are threefold. Through the gifts that give them joy they benefit the ministries and individuals whose lives are touched and transformed in lasting ways. Second, the joy of giving these givers radiate blesses and enriches those who benefit from simply seeing them as mentors, role models, and exemplars. Third, people who are intentionally generous grant blessing to themselves and confirm the biblical promise that the Lord rewards joyful givers with an outpouring of His love (2 Cor. 9:7).

Rolly Samp shares his experience and expertise with us. He is a reliable guide to the necessary steps in personal stewardship and estate planning. This volume has clarity and is comprehensive, but it is not simply a manual for accountants, lawyers, and tax advisers. What sets Samp's work apart is his insight into the motivations and personal satisfactions – the JOYS – of charitable giving. He rightly grasps the spiritual dimensions of being good trustees of our assets. This is why I value this volume so highly. I commend it to you and invite you, too, to savor the joys of giving.

Dr. George K. Brushaber
President, Bethel College and Seminary
Chm. Senior Editors, "Christianity Today"

PRE-WORD

A PRE-WORD

by Rollyn H. Samp, J.D.

20 TRILLION FOR HEIRS

How Much for the Lord?

Christians Forget Churches In Wills

6% Leave Legacy

While baby boomers expect a $2[0] trillion windfall from the estates o[f] their parents during the next 20 yea[rs] the church may not do as well. Bas[ed] on a current national survey of ma[in]line churches, only six percent active churchgoers leave anything their church or its affiliated organ[izations]. That's caused in part by the

Baby Boomers to Inherit Over $20 Trillion

■ Economical Forcast: America marks a historical record with an estimated $20 trillion in estates. What will "baby boomers" do with their inheritance?

65 in the last ten years.

It is estimated that $20 trillion is now held by persons over 65 — the largest fortune held by individuals in the history of the world.

With life expectancies rising, analysts predict within the next 20 years this

the advent of widespread pension plans, 401(k) options and IRAs all fueling a robust economy.

What will baby boomers do with this inheritance? Probably save most of it for anticipated longer lives and rare enjoyment of retirement years. But in inheritance continues to grow, another multi-million in

could be awaiting their children.

Christian Giving Drops to 2% Per Capita Income

■ Economy: With income for Americans at an all time high, giving to churches has dropped to less than two percent per capita income.

Why has this trend continued? The Lilly Foundation funded a three-year study of mainline

- with the rise of consumerism and increased personal debt, smaller amounts of resources are available for personal giving;
- church trends are surprisingly similar across denominational lines;
- church staff are reluctant to educate parishioners in the Biblical principles about the use of money for fear of appearing self-serving.

The founder of a national organization designed to raise the issue of

"Baby Boomers to Inherit $20 Trillion During Next 20 Years"
"76 Million Baby Boomers to Inherit Trillions"
"Christian Giving Drops to 2% of Per-Capita Income"
"6% Leave Legacy – Christians Forget Churches in Wills"

Shocked by these statistics, I was intrigued to learn more why people who have been faithful believers all their lives would be such nominal givers to support the church and its institutions.

Part of the answer came as I read *Behind the Stained Glass Windows: Money Dynamics in the Church* by John and Sylvia Ronsvalle, who summarized The Stewardship Project in book form. The basis for their book was a three-year Lily Foundation-funded interdenominational study of church finance — probably the most in-depth study on the state of financial support for religion in America.

The study had several stunning findings:

- That personal finances — not sex or politics — is the last taboo topic in America.
- That churchgoers view the subject of giving as an extremely private subject.
- Churches have a pre-1950s mind set toward money and haven't provided a positive agenda in an age of affluence.
- With the rise of consumerism and increased personal debt, smaller amounts of resources are available for personal giving.
- Church trends are surprisingly similar across denominational lines.
- Church members now view giving as a fee-for-service responsibility rather than as a biblical imperative.
- Congregations are keeping a higher percentage of income within the congregation compared to previous generations.
- Church staff are reluctant to educate parishioners in the biblical principles about the use of money for fear of appearing self-serving.[1]

[1]Behind the Stained Glass Windows, John and Sylvia Ronsvalle. Baker Books: 1996.

While this study gives statistical insight into why churchgoers give or don't give, it did not probe in detail the relationship between lifelong church giving and gifts to the church and its institutions through estate planning. However, it is apparent many of our personal attitudes currently held on "weekly giving" carry over into an "eternal giving" decision while estate planning.

Does God get back what's been loaned to us? I probed this question further and found that another national study determined only six percent of <u>active</u> churchgoers leave anything to religious institutions in their Wills.

After practicing law for 30 years, I began to reflect on how stewardship related to estate planning in my own practice. For the first 20 years of my practice, clients would rush in asking for a Will, rattling off "we want something simple giving everything equally to the kids" and then rush off after signing. They had completed one of life's most unpleasant tasks in their minds — making a Will.

FAMILY FEUDS WRECK RELATIONSHIPS

But during those years, two profound observations changed my thinking and approach to clients:

First, I noticed that 99 percent of all estate problems were caused by simply stating in Wills, "Divide everything equally among the children." Dad's shotgun, Mom's diamond ring, Aunt Maude's vase, and great-grandpa's immigrant trunk simply can't be divided equally. Distribution of inherited family items is the leading factor in family fights over the average estate. I have developed a technique shared in this book providing tested methods of how to keep children from fighting over the family estate.

With 76 million Baby Boomers about to inherit nearly $20 trillion during the next 20 years, families and family heritage should be strengthened by those who draft Wills to prevent family feuds and to use estate planning as a part of stewardship.

How much is $20 trillion? The total national debt is $5 trillion so potential inheritance is four times our total national debt.

Secondly, I learned by asking the right questions in client interviews that not only did a large percentage of my clients decide to leave something to their churches and other Christian institutions, but they also had a great sense of joy when completing an estate plan.

Their source of joy was a combination of knowing they had returned blessings to the Lord, making clear their gifting intentions and having been good stewards with God's gifts. They were and are witnesses that everything we have is God's and we just get to use it for a short time.

They also experienced peace of mind in having a well-drafted Will which reduced the chance of children or other heirs fighting over their estate, and leaving a lifetime of family scars. They also avoid unnecessary legal bills.

About the same time, I had the opportunity while serving as the church president to work with a leading Christian fund-raiser, Reverend Dr. Rol Kindem. He has a calling to help churches develop and implement giving opportunities for new buildings, renovations, debt retirement and other needs, by his communicating biblically based stewardship.

After learning the principles of biblically based stewardship, I had a chance to participate in communicating the joy of giving as thankfulness for our blessings — rather than an assessment or duty.

THE "TABOO" TOPIC

Why is there such a "taboo" talking about money — particularly how much to contribute to Christian institutions? Why is there such reluctance to discuss estate planning within the church? And why are stewardship and estate planning discussions avoided within families?

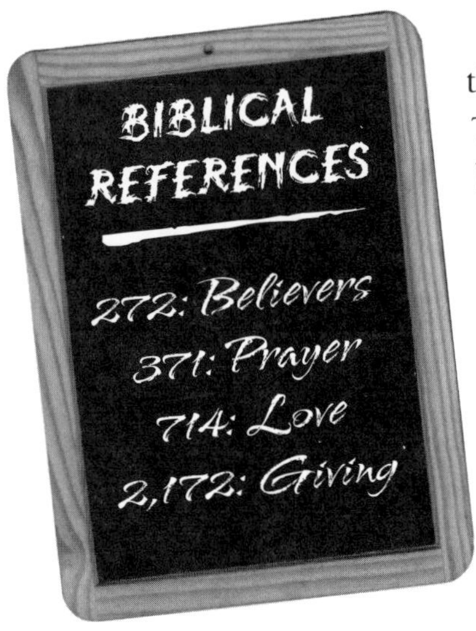

The answers aren't rooted in the quantity of references in the Bible. The Bible has 272 references to believing or believers, 371 references to prayer, 714 references to love or loving, and 2,172 references to possessions or giving, according to Wesley K. Willmer in an address "Stewardship: A Key Link to Commitment and Ministry."[2]

COMMUNICATION EVERYWHERE IS GOING NOWHERE

Part of the answer may be the trend in the last 30 years of declining personal communication. This trend has grown even though the vast array of technical communication options — with cellular phones, pagers, telefax, E-mail, Internet, television and interactive everything — provide an ever-accelerating smorgasbord of communication choices.

But technology has not conquered the numerous barriers to interpersonal communications — between husband and wife, parents and children, siblings, co-workers, and even close friends. We have closed the gap between earth and the moon, Mars and beyond, but too often we struggle to close the gap between two hearts.

In other words, during a time when it is historically and technically possible to have the greatest communication in the history of God's world, people are communicating less and less with each other about faith and family values.

---

[2]Wesley K. Willmer, Stewardship: A Key Link to Commitment and Ministry, Talbot School of Theology, April 5, 1994.

We have closed the gap between earth and the moon, Mars and beyond, but too often we struggle to close the gap between two hearts.

Fear of Rejection

The root of failed communication is found partially in a culturally inspired fear of rejection. This fear traps emotions, thoughts and feelings. We all want to be "in" — drive, wear and eat what's "in" and vacation at "in" places. In fact, each year a variety of publications publish what is "in" and what is "out." Billions of dollars are spent on advertising to influence consumers on what is "in" and what is "out." Subliminally, these advertising messages play on our human fears of rejection. Ironically, many people who want to be close to those they love find themselves isolated, lonely and on the outside of life. We know God is always "in control." However, much of contemporary culture tries to seed doubts that leave us with feelings of rejection, depression, aggression, materialism or other manifestations which leave us feeling "out."

Even basic one-on-one communication can rather simply demonstrate our failures in interpersonal communication. Isn't it easy to ask someone in initial conversation, "How are you doing?" "What do you think about our nice weather?" "Wasn't that a great rain?"

All these are very safe, anti-rejection conversational bits and pieces that require little or no emotion or interpersonal involvement. They seldom lead to any disagreement and, in themselves, cannot bring rejection. You can say "nice day" to an acquaintance passing by with a smile. But try moving up the pyramid of risk or rejection and ask, "How are things at home?" — a high-risk question.

No one would think of asking such a question knowing the chances for total rejection are potentially high, without permission for this kind of conversation with someone we really trust.

Conversation, for most people, even with those we trust, is very difficult when the topics are faith, personal finance, death, and estate planning. To initiate such a conversation means one party must risk rejection or even anger by the other. This is in contrast to the monologues (one-way communication) we experience in education, within families, often within the church, and from television. And it is different from many contemporary conversational exchanges best described as "duologues" — two or more people conversing but not emotionally or sometimes not even connecting on the same subject. The fear of rejection inhibits the majority of people from running these risks.

Over the years of dealing professionally with people unable to communicate about their personal lives, business dealings, or the myriad problems that lead them to a lawyer's office, as a tool of counseling I developed a "Pyramid of Conversational Risks." This demonstrates how communication breaks down.

The "Pyramid of Conversational Risks" provides a visual example of what happens in many contemporary relationships. My experience suggests the risk of rejection rises in direct proportion to the topics ranging from safe to taboo for most people.

Pyramid of Conversational Risks

This "Pyramid of Risks" can vary from person to person and from situation to situation. It depends on personal values, ability to cope with rejection, emotional maturity, fear, interests, education, knowledge of facts and informed opinion.

Many times the root of the fear in discussing a topic is simply lack of knowledge. We tend to avoid things we don't know. Seminars, tapes, and reading materials are good ways to safely lower the "fear of rejection" level. A friend told me years ago "reasonable people, equally informed, seldom disagree." I have found this to be true in the practice of law, which is really the "art of problem-solving." What is important is to get equal information to all parties. Facts should drive decisions while opinions are respected and considered. This helps lower the "risk of rejection" thereby allowing discussion, decision-making, and communication.

END THE FEAR OF REJECTION

Of course, Jesus Christ is the ultimate neutralizer of all rejection. The entire Gospel is the Good News that believers will not be rejected by God. So the fear of rejection can be a spiritual problem as well as a human communication problem. This gives each of us a daily challenge to walk boldly forward in faith knowing that fear is an enemy of Christian witness and that believing in Jesus Christ brings the greatest gift of all — eternal life. It is greater than all of our possessions, all of our good works, and all of our life experiences.

"For God did not give us a spirit of timidity, but a spirit of power, of love and of self- discipline."
— 2 Timothy 1:7.

It is my experience that a major barrier to Christian stewardship and estate planning is a lack of knowledge, coupled with a lack of communication that fails to bring believers to a decision or even a discussion of their personal estate choices. Without the proper tools to have a meaningful discussion, rejection or avoidance of the topic takes place — not unlike the fear of leading a Bible study without taking time to prepare for it.

I decided ten years ago, whether it cost me clients or not, I would enter into the "taboo" zone of Christian dialogue and broach the subject of giving to the church and its institutions as part of estate planning. And happily, I can say I have never lost a client because of witnessing in this unique way. What I have seen is a peace of mind which comes from knowing that written in the last legal document anyone will read from an individual is a reflection of his Christian values, a written testament of his faith, and his personal decision regarding the gifts he will leave on this earth.

Has The Government Written Your Will?

Another astounding fact confirming a general lack of communication on estate planning is that fewer than 30 percent of Americans have even bothered to make a Will. The other 70 percent have allowed the government to write a Will and distribute their lifetime accumulations according to statutory formulas which vary from state to state. Of course, no one without a Will or some other estate planning device will ever leave anything to church or charity because that is not provided for in the law. In fact, for persons without heirs who have no Wills, their entire estates will go to the government. These people will never give themselves the opportunity to consider a "final tithe."

If you have not done a Will, here's a sample of what the government has provided for you:

Last Will and Testament

The State on behalf of __(your name)__ hereby grants all personal and real property as follows by State law since __(your name)__ did not write a Will.

After all funeral and last illness expenses are paid, all real and personal property shall be disposed of as follows: (one will be checked)[3]

____ If you have a surviving spouse and all of the decedent's children are also children of the surviving spouse, then the estate passes to the surviving spouse.

____ If you have a surviving spouse and one or more of the decedent's children are not descendants of the surviving spouse (for example, in situations of divorce, remarriage or second marriages), then the estate is divided as follows:

The first $100,000 plus one-half of any balance of the estate to the surviving spouse, with the balance distributed to the decedent's children.

____ If no surviving spouse or children, distribution is by law of lineal succession.

____ If you are divorced, have adopted children, no children or other close heirs, the government has special provisions for you.

____ If you are survived only by minor children, the court will select who will raise them.

____ Nothing may be given to church or charity.

BY THE STATE ON YOUR BEHALF

____

[3]Distribution may vary by state law.

However, if you do not have a properly drawn estate plan, you should not feel bad . . . unless you fail to get one. The late Chief Justice Warren Burger of the United States Supreme Court died with a poorly drafted Will that cost his heirs over $400,000. He wrote his own Will on a computer missing many of the basic elements of estate planning. While he was a brilliant jurist, drafting estate plans was not something he was accustomed to doing. In fact, there were numerous misspellings in the Will suggesting it was done in haste and without spell checking. Perhaps he was still grieving the loss of his wife, since the Will was drafted shortly after her death. But in that case he violated Lincoln's admonition: "A lawyer who serves as his own counsel has a fool for a client."

It is hard to be objective when working on something as emotional and personal as an estate plan. So the first question to be answered before thinking about stewardship in estate planning is —

Do I need a Will?

The answer is quite simple: Do you like the Will your state has prepared for you by law or do you want a Will drafted that clearly reflects your wishes?

At this point a cynical thought might be, "There goes another lawyer looking for business." In my seminars I tell people the advantages of using an attorney to properly draft a Will, but there are "home remedies" for writing a Will such as kits or handwritten holographic Wills which are legal in many states. While these do-it-yourself options are not generally recommended and virtually never address stewardship in estate planning, disliking attorneys is not a good reason to miss the opportunity to be a good steward of the gifts God has given you and to celebrate the joy of giving through your Will.

And neither is the cost of having a Will drafted a good excuse for not having one. The average cost for drafting a simple Will is

$150.00 in our office. This is not a large cost to be sure a lifetime of earnings and possessions are properly distributed without a family fight or as prescribed by law. A well-crafted Will provides the opportunity for a final thank you for the gifts each of us has been given by God.

There are other choices for estate planning rather than a simple Will. Couples currently exceeding $1.35 million in net worth need a more complex Will if they wish to avoid federal estate tax. *Congress and states have had numerous plans to change estate and inheritance taxes, so following legal changes is important as a part of good stewardship.*

Some Christians question whether legal tax avoidance is good stewardship. Christ said:

> "Then give to Caesar what is Caesar's, and to God what is God's."
> — Luke 20:25

The fact is, Congress, by exempting from tax all gifts to qualified churches and related institutions, has a government policy of encouraging people to legally give to these entities. Therefore, using the various tools Congress has provided is secular support for being a good steward.

There are also combinations of living trusts, charitable annuities, Dynasty Trusts™ and life insurance which can be important estate planning tools, along with complex estate plans tailored to fit family needs and choices.

Just like a decision to buy a new car can be a lengthy family decision, once the decision is made there are multiple choices and options to tailor the new car to fit the family's desires. Several options to consider are summarized in later chapters. But frankly, all estate planning choices are incomplete unless there is a commitment to experience the joy of thankful Christian giving through estate planning.

It took me years to reach this point. Your taking a few minutes to walk with me through the questions and choices you have as a blessed person could be a milestone in your life. You should not feel judged based on giving as you think about what you want to leave as your Christian legacy. You cannot buy your way into heaven, so leaving something for the Lord's work is not an airplane ticket to everlasting salvation. Belief in Christ is the only means of salvation. But if it fits a discussion within your family on the importance of lifelong stewardship, then our moments together through this book will be worth your time. By your decision, Christ's work through his servants will continue to benefit.

We Are Blessed

We've been blessed beyond measure the past 50 years in America. We have not had famine, war on our soil or plagues to disturb our lifestyle. This does not ignore the problems of poverty, homelessness, health or financial problems. But given the support of taxpayers in America, the least a household can have today on public assistance with a combination of money, food stamps and rent subsidies is an amount equal to approximately $15,000 per year, plus access to medical treatment. When compared to the other 6 billion people in the world, America's poorest of poor are still among the one percent wealthiest in the world.

And the average household income in America today of $37,277.60 puts many families in the .01 percent of the wealthiest in the world.

We all live better than the richest people in history thanks to the opportunities for advanced medical care, technological convenience, low food costs as a percentage of family income, extraordinary mobility and luxuries beyond anyone's dreams … even 50 years ago.

We are a blessed people in terms of possessions and economic freedom. We even have a security net for retirement and medical care which, even with its potential flaws and problems, will provide a comfortable life within the context of world history for every American.

But the question of how we have responded by giving only two percent of our per-capita earnings to churches during a given year and with only six percent of active church participants planning to leave any of their over-$20 trillion in wealth to the church is a perplexing question given the biblical mandate to be good stewards of what we have received. We even sing hymns of giving on Sunday, such as "We Give Thee But Thine Own."

We Give Thee

We give Thee but Thine own,
Whate'er the gift may be:
All that we have is Thine alone,
A trust, O Lord, from Thee.

— William W. How, 1854

It is my prayer each person would set aside past feelings about lawyers, estates, the institutional church or whatever barrier has made the discussion of your gifts to God "taboo" and reflect on the blessings and opportunities we each have through our final words to make a lasting statement of faith, joy and thankfulness.

— Rollyn H. Samp, Founder
Fellowship of Christian Estate Planners

For God so
loved the
world that
he gave

his one
and only Son,
that whoever
believes in
him shall
not perish
but have
eternal life.

JOHN 3:16

WHAT DOES THE BIBLE SAY ABOUT GIVING?

Giving

"Give, and it will be given to you. A good measure, pressed down, shaken together and running over, will be poured into your lap. For with the measure you use, it will be measured to you."
— *Luke 6:38*

CHAPTER 1

We are born into this world with nothing. We are each given different talents and possessions to use while on earth. But we leave this world with nothing — just as we came into life. Recently, a multi-billionaire corporate president died. After the funeral one acquaintance asked of another, "How much did he leave?" "He left it all," was the answer.

Death is blind to the rich and famous, poor and unknown, and all in between. Everyone "leaves it all" upon passing from this world. The world would say Princess Diana, John F. Kennedy Jr., Elvis Presley, John Lennon, and hundreds of other so-called "superstars" of contemporary society had it all.

Their real epitaph should read "They left it all."

Factually, we can show Americans are better off by looking at real income (adjusted for inflation) which has gone from $1,501 annual per capita income in 1950 to $25,660 today — an increase of over 1,700 percent.

Today, discretionary income has grown, allowing average Americans to have 11.2 percent of family income for personal spending choices beyond essential living. These choices have led to the highest standard of housing, food, cars, personal conveniences, travel, recreation and clothing in the history of the world.

One other major factor dominates family income in America. We have a tax system which inherently encourages the accumulation of wealth in farms, ranches, family businesses and retirement portfolios. In other words, much of our wealth or net worth can be "paper wealth" rather than available funds. So many families have growing balance sheets but continue to have the same annual income to make spending choices.

The accumulation of wealth is motivated in part by uncertainty in retirement costs, protection against extraordinary health care expenses, and a desire to make life easier for children than parents have had throughout the 20th century.

STEWARDSHIP

These are all important motivations and can be included as good stewardship by planning to be as self-sufficient as possible.

But good stewardship does not diminish the ability to accomplish personal financial goals by sharing our wealth with the church and its institutions — on a weekly or other regular basis and by leaving a portion of our life's accumulations through a stewardship-based estate plan.

A "final tithe" is no substitute for regular giving. The "final tithe" is a gift from estates at death — not the important daily commitment to being good stewards of our lives and possessions.

What are the principles of stewardship?

Each believer can make that determination by reflecting on what the Bible says about our giving. The Old Testament has some clear principles relating to a "tithe" — giving the first 10 percent to God. The New Testament has additional guidance on giving to the Lord. And many religious leaders, while clearly telling believers any giving is a personal decision, will suggest a "tithe" is a good place to start when considering what level of giving is appropriate.

The Bible does not require any final gift to buy a "fire insurance" policy and that is not the message of this book. It is designed to help Christians refocus on the biblical basis of stewardship, apply it to the tools of estate planning and offer the choices people can make in their giving both now and in their final gifts.

There is no magical formula. There is no requirement. There are only the blessings of giving and realizing the peace that comes from your decision to include a "final tithe" in your Will or trust.

And if you have any question of how people are blessed by giving, simply ask a known giver to Christian needs: "I know you're a great supporter of Christian needs. Have you been blessed by your giving?"

The answer will simply astound you.

Tithing — the Old Testament rule of giving — has a variety of references including:

"Speak to the Israelites and say to them: 'When you enter the land I am going to give you and you reap its harvest, bring to the priest a sheaf of the first grain you harvest.'" — Leviticus 23:10.

The "first fruits" concept is simply the idea of giving back to God the best of what he has given us. Personal financial planners use a similar concept in designing retirement plans as well. They urge a "pay yourself first" concept of putting 10 percent into savings for future personal needs, retirement, and to guard against financial emergencies. Good stewardship would suggest "give to God first."

The Old Testament continues its guide to giving:

"'and now I bring the firstfruits of the soil that you, O Lord, have given me.' Place the basket before the Lord your God and bow down before him." — Deuteronomy 26:10.

Not only is the giving important, but also having a heart matching the gift is necessary.

And there is a promise of great blessings to those who give with their hearts:

"'Bring the whole tithe into the storehouse, that there may be food in my house. Test me in this,' says the Lord Almighty, 'and see if I will not throw open the flood-gates of heaven and pour out so much blessing that you will not have room enough for it.'" — Malachi 3:10.

So the question becomes: If we put at least 10 percent toward the work of the Lord and 10 percent into personal savings, can we live each month on the other 80 percent? This is where families need to cross the taboo communication barrier of discussing personal finances and estate planning.

The New Testament reflects no law of tithing. In fact, Jesus chides those who give with the wrong motives:

> *"Woe to you, teachers of the law and Pharisees, you hypocrites! You give a tenth of your spices — mint, dill and cummin. But you have neglected the more important matters of the law — justice, mercy and faithfulness. You should have practiced the latter, without neglecting the former."* — Matthew 23:23.

But the New Testament reflects a message of stewardship in a very positive way. A steward is one who manages for an owner. Christian stewardship acknowledges that everything belongs to the Lord; not just 10 percent. We are challenged to manage all He has given, rich or poor, from the widow's mite to the billionaire's portfolio.

We are challenged to manage all He has given, rich or poor, from the widow's mite to the billionaire's portfolio.

The New Testament is helpful in understanding stewardship in the following passages:

Stewardship is proportionate to income:

Each Christian is called to give according to his means: "For I testify that they gave as much as they were able, and even beyond their ability. Entirely on their own, they urgently pleaded with us for the privilege of sharing in this service to the saints." — 2 Corinthians 8:3-4.

Stewardship is an attitude of giving to God the GIFT OF OURSELVES:

"And they did not do as we expected, but they gave themselves first to the Lord and then to us in keeping with God's will." — 2 Corinthians 8:5.

It is a sign of the genuineness of our love:

"But just as you excel in everything — in faith, in speech, in knowledge, in complete earnestness and in your love for us — see that you also excel in this grace of giving. I am not commanding you, but I want to test the sincerity of your love by comparing it with the earnestness of others." — 2 Corinthians 8:7-8.

And it is based on what we have been given:

"For if the willingness is there, the gift is acceptable according to what one has, not according to what he does not have." — 2 Corinthians 8:12.

Stewardship includes thanks:

"This service that you perform is not only supplying the needs of God's people but is also overflowing in many expressions of thanks to God." — 2 Corinthians 9:12.

Stewardship requires a commitment:

A "final tithe" is such a promise and given willingly: "So I thought it necessary to urge the brothers to visit you in advance and finish the arrangements for the generous gift you had promised. Then it will be ready as a generous gift, not as one grudgingly given."
— 2 Corinthians 9:5.

Stewardship is a challenge to our faith in the promises of God — that we will reap as we sow:

"Remember this: Whoever sows sparingly will also reap sparingly, and whoever sows generously will also reap generously. Each man should give what he has decided in his heart to give, not reluctantly or under compulsion, for God loves a cheerful giver. And God is able to make all grace abound to you, so that in all things at all times, having all that you need, you will abound in every good work. As it is written:

'He has scattered abroad his gifts to the poor;
his righteousness endures forever.'

"Now he who supplies seed to the sower and bread for food will also supply and increase your store of seed and will enlarge the harvest of your righteousness. You will be made rich in every way so that you can be generous on every occasion, and through us your generosity will result in thanksgiving to God."
— 2 Corinthians 9:6-11.

Lasting stewardship is a way to glorify God:

*"Because of the service by which you have proved yourselves, men will praise God for the obedience that accompanies your confession of the gospel of Christ, and for your generosity in sharing with them and with everyone else."
— 2 Corinthians 9:13.*

Christians should not be bound by the rules of the Old Testament with the legalism of the tithe. Instead, we are challenged to give according to four New Testament guidelines. Christian giving should be:

Proportionally to one's income
(1 Corinthians 16:2, 2 Corinthians 8:12)
Consistently *(1 Corinthians 16:2)*
Sacrificially *(Mark 12:43-44, 2 Corinthians 8:2-3)*
Cheerfully *(2 Corinthians 9:7)*

So the concept of a "final tithe" is not a fixed formula for giving through estates. It is a great discussion point to apply the historic basis of Old Testament giving with the Good News of asking stewards of God's blessings to give proportionally, consistently, sacrificially, and cheerfully. Accepting this opportunity to give through Christian estate planning can lead to the blessing of knowing for eternity that whatever you decide to leave for the continuation of the Lord's work will be your real and lasting legacy.

If you remain in me and my words remain in you, ask whatever you wish, and it will be given you. This is to my Father's glory, that you bear much fruit, showing yourselves to be my disciples.

John 15:7-8

What if every active Christian family made a decision to make a ten percent tithe gift to our Lord at the end of their lives?

Vision TO SEE

"I never met a man who consistently tested out the promises of God and found they did not work"
-GLENN CLARK

What equals Sixty Billion Dollars Annually?

10%

How much money is One Trillion Dollars?

Faith TO BELIEVE

THE TitHE

10%

The wise man looks ahead.

Courage TO ACT

10%

MAN'S MIND STRETCHED BY A NEW IDEA NEVER GOES BACK TO ITS ORIGINAL DIMENSION!

WHAT IF EVERY BELIEVER TITHED?

Believing

"One man gives freely, yet gains even more; another withholds unduly, but comes to poverty. A generous man will prosper; he who refreshes others will himself be refreshed."
— *Proverbs 11:24-25*

CHAPTER 2

"And now, brothers, we want you to know about the grace that God has given the Macedonian churches. Out of the most severe trial, their overflowing joy and their extreme poverty welled up in rich generosity. For I testify that they gave as much as they were able, and even beyond their ability. Entirely on their own, they urgently pleaded with us for the privilege of sharing in this service to the saints. And they did not do as we expected, but they gave themselves first to the Lord and then to us in keeping with God's will. So we urged Titus, since he had earlier made a beginning, to bring also to completion this act of grace on your part. But just as you excel in everything — in faith, in speech, in knowledge, in complete earnestness and in your love for us — see that you also excel in this grace of giving." — 2 Corinthians 8:1-7

Total giving by Americans currently amounts to approximately $175 billion a year. Of that, the category of "religion" gets about 40 percent. But this represents only two percent of our per capita income. In fact, twice as much money is spent on tobacco and alcoholic beverages by American families ($152 billion annually) than all religious giving.

With only two percent of annual per-capita income going to support churches and only six percent of active Christians remembering the Church and its institutions in their Wills, the opportunity to generate ongoing support for ministries and Christian organizations is staggering.

While this should not be the motive for making a "final tithe," it is an element of good stewardship to consider what would happen if every active Christian family made a decision to make a gift to our Lord at life's end. For hypothetical purposes, we will use the 10 percent guideline to demonstrate the possibilities.

Assuming $20 trillion transfers in inheritance during the next 20 years and half of the wealth is held by Christians, that would amount to $10 trillion being passed through Christian families.

NO CHANGE IN GIFTING

If there is no increase in current final gifting, the following would be the projected amount received by Christian organizations:

- It is estimated $10 trillion will transfer by inheritance between years 2000-2020 from believers.

12 billion dollars

- Assuming six percent of Christians leave two percent of their estates to the church and its institutions, total gifting to Christian needs by Wills will be roughly $12 billion.

Now look at the possibilities if active Christian families were to consider a "final tithe" during the same period:

- If $10 trillion transfers by inheritance during the next 20 years,
- and if every believer passing away in the next 20 years would leave a 10 percent "final tithe,"

1 trillion dollars

- total gifting to Christian needs by Wills would be an estimated $1 trillion. This is compared to the $12 billion currently being given through Wills and Trusts.

If $1 trillion were endowed to churches or Christian organizations, colleges, seminaries and missions, and only the interest spent, with a six percent assumed rate of return, this would generate $60 billion annually for local churches and other Christian needs throughout America and around the world. Remember, this is just having the interest of "final tithes" available for our Lord's continuing work each year.

How Much Money is $1 Trillion?

It is a sum equal to:

- nearly 3,450 new B-1 bombers
- building 58 international space stations
- producing 4,890 *Titanic*-type mega movies
- buying over 1.15 million fully loaded new Corvettes

And $60 Billion a Year in Interest Income is Equal to:

- the amount needed to raise 328,415 American children from birth to adulthood
- the Yankees' baseball team payroll for 905 years

- the purchase price of 27,281,290 acres of Iowa farmland
- the cost of all cardiac bypasses done in the United States for 11 years
- 210,084,000 one-way airline tickets from New York to Los Angeles
- the budget of New York City for 1.6 years
- the cost of food for one year for 10,414,496 U.S. families
- 304,878 model year 2000 John Deere combines
- the purchase price of 143,940 McDonald's franchises
- the cost of over 400,000,000 pair of Nike athletic shoes

A Breakdown in Giving

Let's assume "final tithers" were to divide 10 percent of their estates by leaving one-third to their congregations; one-third to Christian colleges, seminaries, or Christian outreach programs; and one-third to other important national and international Christian work for missions, medical assistance, disaster relief, hunger, evangelism, music ministries, television outreach, housing, Bible distribution, or several hundred other great ministries that fit a giver's choice.

Assume the money is willed so only interest could be used for this work. Using an assumption that giving is factored for a ten-year average, the following possibilities are created:

One-Third to Local Churches

If these gifts created $170 billion in endowment gifts to 350,000 churches, there would be roughly *$485,000* average gifts per church earning a six percent return per year on the funds. This would provide an average of nearly *$30,000 per church each year for local ministry*.

One-Third to Christian Colleges, Seminaries, Christian Social Organizations

If another $170 billion were divided by just 1,000 Christian educational institutions, the funds earning six percent a year would equal nearly *$10 million per entity per year.*

One-Third for Other Christian Work

And there are over 600,000 Christian charities in America. The top 25 carry out roughly half of the major Christian work around the world. $170 billion divided by these 25 leading Christian worldwide entities would give each *$5.4 billion a year* in endowment income. And the other approximately 600,000 Christian charities would have an additional $5.4 billion to divide for their work.

Considering $75 million is currently given annually to these organizations, the idea of a "final tithe" from active Christians today offers tremendous possibilities for the future.

The decision for individual Christians to make a stewardship commitment in their estate planning is a personal choice. But these calculations demonstrate the kind of financial possibilities that could be generated for the 21st century church by giving with a renewed commitment to stewardship.

While the illustrations used are broad averages, the challenge of making a "final tithe" proportional to one's net estate, sacrificial to the extent of a faith statement, and cheerfully knowing the fruits of your labor will continue working beyond your time on earth, are exciting. Certainly, with the biblical guidance on giving and the great promise in celebrating the joy of giving, this is worthy of discussion within the family of believers.

Believe

"... those who hope in the Lord will renew their strength. They will soar on wings like eagles;"

ISAIAH 40:31

NOTES/ QUESTIONS
1. How to fairly divide heirlooms....
2. How much will I have to live on?
3. If the kids divorce how will that affect their inheritance....?
4. If I must go into a nursing home (last resort..!) how will the state take my money?
5. Should I have a trust? If so- how done? Cost?
6. How does hubby's retirement funds figure in the picture?
7. Don't want to be kept alive by machines - what is the best way to prevent that? IMPORTANT
8. How do I arrange for funds to go to my alma mater?
9. What is probate - how does it affect inheritance as far as time? (When kids get $....)
10. Say I live beyond my expected years - will there be money enough to support me?
11. Explain inheritance tax...
12. How is competency decided & who decides.....?

Choice

HOW SPOUSES CAN DECIDE WHAT TO GIVE

"… remembering the words the Lord Jesus himself said: 'It is more blessed to give than to receive.'"
— Acts 20:35

CHAPTER 3

The decision to do any estate planning usually begins with one spouse deciding they "need a Will." A lawyer is called and an appointment is scheduled. Unlike doctors, most attorneys do not advertise their specialties. Therefore, clients may not know for sure if they are getting estate planning from an attorney who is skilled in this area of the law. Most attorneys today specialize in a specific legal area. While all have had basic courses in Will drafting and estate planning, the chances of getting a criminal lawyer who may be too embarrassed to tell a neighbor or friend the last Will he drew was for a law school Wills class may be more frequent than rare.

The first question when calling a lawyer's office should be: "Is estate planning a substantial part of Lawyer Jones's law practice? If not: Could you recommend two or three lawyers who do this type of work?"

WHY DON'T PEOPLE GET WILLS?

But getting to the point of even making the phone call means the "taboo" barrier of discussing death and estate plans has been reached by people who have decided to do some form of estate planning.

Some studies have been done on why people avoid estate planning. The research suggests the decision to get a Will is a subliminal acknowledgment of mortality; of getting old and not wanting to face the reality of not living forever. Others find that the inability of spouses to agree on an estate plan is another reason to avoid getting a Will. Fear of attorneys and horror stories of probating estates are other reasons for Will avoidance. And ignorance of the consequences of not having a Will is yet another factor. Still others feel when they commit to a Will they are giving up control over their decisions and funds, even though the opposite is true.

If there is harmony within the family now, why face potential disharmony by tackling such a seemingly difficult subject as estate planning? It could mean facing unpleasant problems within a family. Likewise, with so many blended families today, sorting out who gets what and when can be a challenge.

With potentially 500 television channels at our disposal, the world at our fingertips via the Internet or telephone, and several million videos to rent for home viewing plus tens of thousands of other entertainment choices, why would anyone want to set aside time to talk about an estate plan?

Since less than 30 percent of Americans have any kind of estate plan, those who do tend to fall into one of the following categories:

Fear of illness

- A spouse is faced with a terminal illness or traumatic health event and the couple decides they need to "get their affairs in order."

Fear of the tax collector

- A life insurance agent, bank loan or trust officer, or tax preparer has suggested without a Will the government "could take a large bite out of your estate." In fear of the tax collector, they pick the lesser of two evils and "see a lawyer."

Fear of airplane crash

- Families planning a vacation trip and taking an airplane flight are another category of those who decide to "get a Will." While the odds are 1 in 250,000 of dying on a commercial airplane flight and 115 people die each day in car accidents (one every 13 minutes). The prospect of flying as a family still generates a concern for having a completed estate plan.

Fear of the unknown

- Others attend a seminar on elder law in one form or another and are convinced they "need to do something."

Parents with young families

- Young parents concerned about who might raise their children if they were both killed are among the faithful in getting a "young family" Will. They may have very little net worth but take steps to protect their children's economic future with life insurance and to decide on a guardian if they were both deceased. This eliminates a Court having to choose a guardian for their children in the catastrophic event they lose their parents.

Divorced parents with minor children

- Divorced parents with minor children also tend to get Wills to address child custody issues.

Well-organized people who plan ahead

- Lastly, there are people who are well-organized and plan ahead who have done estate planning. They realize the benefits of a well-planned future. They know a Will is a flexible document that can be changed and have decided to get on paper their wishes and needs.

Whatever keeps people from doing estate planning raises serious questions of stewardship. If you believe that everything you have is a gift from God and your opportunity on earth is to manage it, the question becomes whether you are a good steward by not having an estate plan which reflects your care and custody of what you have been given.

The author of *Peter Pan*, Sir James Barrie, wrote a play years ago called "The Will." In the play, a husband and wife go to a lawyer to prepare a Will. But the lawyer cannot draft the Will because the couple forbids ever mentioning the word "death" or any phrases to suggest the husband will not live forever.

This is the ultimate example of being unable to confront the reality that everyone is mortal.

Having a concept of Christian stewardship and the role estate planning can play in being a good steward can relieve many of the obstacles of seeking advice on "how to complete a Christian estate plan."

A Typical Trip to the Lawyer

A snapshot of one couple visiting a lawyer to "get a Will done" might illuminate a typical attempt at estate planning. It goes something like this:

Henry and Emma have scheduled an appointment with an attorney they know who lives down the street. They are casual acquaintances but not close friends. An assistant ushers the couple into the lawyer's office. The lawyer steps around his massive desk to greet the couple.

"Henry and Emma, nice to see you. Can we get you a cup of coffee?" he asks while directing them to chairs opposite his desk.

They agree to accept the coffee. "Could I have cream with mine?" Emma asks.

The lawyer returns to his professional perch behind his desk and awaits his secretary to bring the coffee.

"Boy, the weather's been hot and humid, hasn't it?"

Henry agrees. But he is sitting with his arms crossed and is not prepared to be very talkative. "Yep. Not like last year when it rained most of the time."

"I see you folks coming and going a lot. Have you been traveling?" the lawyer asks.

"Don't we wish," Emma offers. "Henry's got cancer and we've been doctoring for the past four months."

The lawyer is momentarily frozen in his escalation up the pyramid of risks in conversation. "Well, I hope things are going better for you," he offers sympathetically.

"The doctors say it's under control for now, but it's not good," Emma relates.

By now Henry is sitting stiff as a board. He doesn't want to talk about his cancer, his estate or even be in a lawyer's office. He's thinking that if the doctors haven't already taken all the blood they need from him, the lawyer will finish the task.

"We think we'd better get a Will because we don't know what's going to happen," Emma continues.

"Well, a Will is a good idea. To help you get what you want, I'd like to run through a little checklist with you that will help me," the lawyer offers.

"How much is this going to cost?" Henry asks breaking his silence.

"It depends on how complicated it is," replies the lawyer.

"We want the simplest thing you got. Everything to my wife while she lives and then the rest equally divided between the kids," he instructs.

"Because of tax laws, I assume you'll want to legally avoid as much tax as possible with this," the lawyer suggests.

"Absolutely. That's why we came here, 'cause we don't want the government taking our hard-earned money," Henry says.

"Let me run through my checklist and we'll see how simple we can make this." The lawyer proceeds to work through his form that matches his computer program to produce a "simple Will" — names, Social Security numbers, names of the children, birth dates, any grandchildren . . . "Can you folks tell me what you own and what you owe?"

"We don't owe anything. Everything's paid for," Emma replies. "Henry, what do we own?"

"Well, we've got the house, both have cars, my pension, some IRA's and some other money, plus Emma inherited part of a farm with her brother out west." Henry is unwilling to reveal the details of his finances. In fact, he's been keeping all the books and records and has not even shared how much they have with Emma.

Emma diverts the conversation. "We pay a lot of income tax every year. Why, they even tax our Social Security now."

The lawyer now has a clue that Henry and Emma may have

accumulated more in assets than their $150,000 three-bedroom home would reveal. The lawyer tries again. "I don't need exact numbers or types of investments for this discussion, but if we totaled up the value of all your assets today and sold them, what would they be worth?"

"We're not planning to sell," Henry retorts. "We just want a Will."

"No, I'm not saying you would sell anything. I'm just trying to figure out which type of Will we need that would be best for you."

Henry does not relent. "We want a simple Will. Not something filled with lawyer gobbeldy-goop."

"Here's the problem. If you have over $1 million in net worth, we need to use a marital deduction Will to avoid federal estate tax," the lawyer offers.

Henry is still uncomfortable about sharing his net worth. "I suppose if you took everything and the way things are going today with the crazy prices people pay for things, we'd be over $1 million."

"Could you give me a ballpark of how much over?"

"Well, I haven't really totaled it up. I bought an annuity that probably isn't involved. The house is in joint tenancy so my wife gets it and I put her name and the kids' on the CDs and stocks."

By now, the lawyer knows he has a complex estate, but his client doesn't believe the estate is complex. The client just wants to sign something and get out of the office placating his wife that he now has a Will. The lawyer continues trying to explain the potential problem in the current titling of property if the couple wants to avoid federal estate tax.

Henry again says, "I thought the law said everything going to a spouse is tax free."

"That's correct; but if we don't legally utilize your allowed tax exclusion, there can be an estate tax on your wife's estate," the lawyer advises.

"Well, let her figure that out. They'll probably change the laws ten times by then. Just draw something giving everything to her and everything equally to the kids when she's gone," he instructs.

The lawyer completes his questionnaire with Emma supplying the information on the three kids and four grandchildren. The lawyer agrees to draft a simple Will and then a marital deduction Will so the couple can see the difference in rough draft. "With the computers, we can change this any time," he offers. "I really am going to have to write a cover letter explaining the differences and why you should consider a marital deduction Will."

Henry is ready to leave. "Go ahead and draft what you think, but let's get this done."

Emma interrupts, "You know, we have one child who's handicapped and gets a government check each month."

Now the lawyer is near exasperation. He's working on a complex estate that his clients think is simple.

"With a handicapped child we can draft a special trust so she keeps all her government benefits, plus her share of your estate can be used for life enhancement."

"Well, go ahead and put that in too," Henry says getting up to leave.

"But whom do you want to administer the estate? What happens if that individual can't? And if something happened to your kids, how would their share of the estate be handled?"

"Just leave those things blank and we'll talk about them later," Henry replies. "I'm not feeling that well and I really don't want a big legal mess with all this."

"That's what we're trying to avoid. But let me put all this in writing with some rough drafts and then we can do a follow-up meeting to see what you really need," the lawyer offers.

"Okay, but remember to keep it simple. And I don't want a big bill for something that you should be able to just run off on a computer and have us sign."

The lawyer gets up and shakes the couple's hands as they leave. He puts his notes in a file and starts returning phone calls, hoping words of wisdom will eventually come to communicate with Henry and Emma that they have several lifelong issues needing to be resolved if they really want to protect their estate and give everything equally to their children.

> **"Well, it's hard for a mere man to believe that woman doesn't have equal rights."**
>
> — Dwight D. Eisenhower

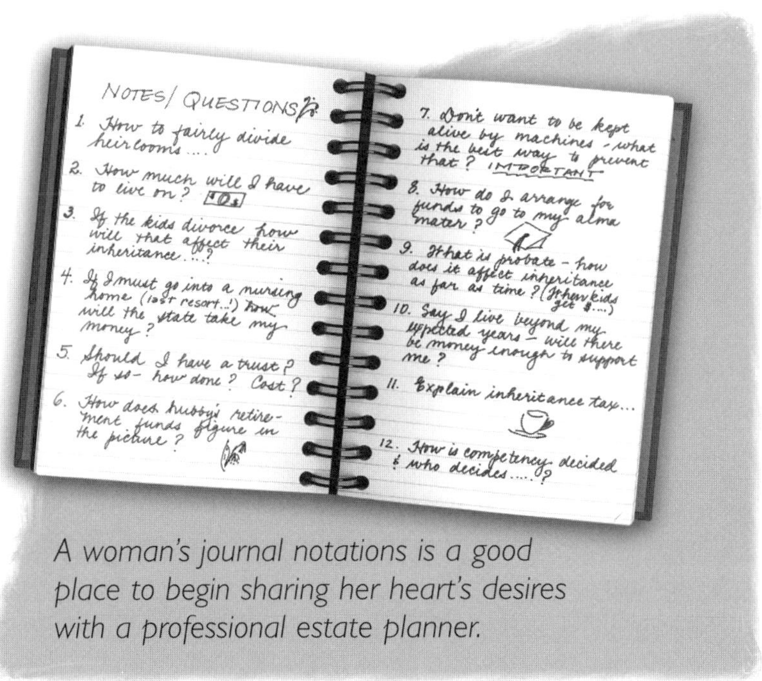

A woman's journal notations is a good place to begin sharing her heart's desires with a professional estate planner.

ANOTHER COUPLE

Now let's take another snapshot of a different couple. Juan and Maria have both been thinking about getting an estate plan for some time. They happen to call a different office for an appointment — one specializing in Christian Estate Planning.

Upon their arrival, a personal assistant greets them and immediately takes them to her office to complete a basic questionnaire with all the vital information. This is done for efficiency, allowing the attorney's time to be spent working directly with the client, and improves accuracy by having all family details available in one place and ready for entry into the computer. It also aids in the general discussion of estates. The assistant then brings the clients into the attorney's office.

The clients are greeted and seated around a comfortable table — more of a family-meeting-around-the-dinner-table setting.

"What time's your dentist appointment?" the attorney asks.

"We don't have a dentist appointment," Maria responds.

"Oh, I thought if you had to see both a lawyer and a dentist the same day, you'd really be having a terrible day," he says with a smile.

The ice is broken. Scanning the questionnaire, the lawyer asks about their kids and grandchildren as they are listed. Both of them give the details on how the kids are doing, when they see them, and perhaps an upcoming trip.

"You're in a select group. You know, only 30 percent of Americans have bothered to do any kind of estate planning. The messes the other 70 percent leave are an attorney's dream," the attorney adds.

"We thought it was time to get something done, but we're not sure what," Maria offers.

"The process is fairly simple. If we can discuss your goals on how you want your money and possessions handled after you're gone, we can draft something that clearly reflects your wishes," he says.

"We just want it simple. No gobbledygoop," Juan says.

"We can do that, and what we draft I want you to clearly understand before you sign; but we do need to be sure this document reflects your current wishes. I say that because a Will can be changed any time as long as you live and are competent, so what we should work on is how you'd like things handled if something happened to you now. Of course, we need to check to see which type of Will best fits your needs because of federal tax laws. If you totaled everything you own and deducted everything you owe, would you have a combined net worth of over $2 million?" the attorney asks.

"No, we're not in that league," Juan chuckles.

"I have to ask because there are types of Wills and trusts that can keep your money within the family and give you choices rather than letting the government get it. Do you think you might inherit or have a substantial amount of money coming that would push you to the level the federal government would tax?" the attorney asks.

"No, our family comes from hard-working, God-fearing people who were able to own a house, pay their bills, give the kids an education, and enjoy retirement," Maria offers.

The discussion on the Will proceeds to talking about handicapped trusts for any disabled heirs, who would inherit what if one or more of their children passed away before them, and who would administer their Will.

The attorney shares an example: "We have four children. And this table we're sitting around was my great-grandfather's. It was the only good thing he brought, along with a plow and oxen, to his sod house on his newly acquired homestead. Now, how am I going to divide this equally among four kids?"

The discussion flows on to the family treasures that are hard to divide and the hard feelings that develop in families when two daughters try to divide mother's wedding ring equally. The attorney offers five methods to prevent family feuds, and the conversation becomes much easier as Juan and Maria clearly understand the desire of a lawyer to prevent family feuds in estate planning. They decide to think about two of the choices and make a final decision when they get the rough drafts of the Will.

At this point, the attorney feels like he's known the family for years as within an hour they've had a very good exchange of sensitive information on the family estate and have alleviated most of their concerns. The attorney then crosses into the highest area of conversational risk with a client.

"There's one more idea I'd like to share with you. If you decide this is something you'd like to pursue after you've thought about it and discussed it, we can put this into your Will," he offers.

"I see you've been involved with your church and you may have other Christian organizations or groups that are important to you. In America, a lot of our wealth gets built up in savings accounts, retirement accounts, or dozens of other ways. It's estimated in the next 20 years $20 trillion or more of this money will pass to heirs. Tragically, other surveys show that within three years, 80 percent of all lump sums received by heirs is spent. I'm not talking specifically about your kids or your family. But consider how much churches and church-related groups could benefit if everyone left a little in their Will for the Lord's work," the attorney shares.

"I have many clients who have decided to leave a 'final tithe' — 90 percent to their kids and 10 percent to support Christian work. Many have given a larger percentage to continuing Christ's work. And I've had 100 percent who have done this express a sense of joy in making this decision. It doesn't matter if an estate is large or small. That final gift is a tremendous faith statement some people like to make. And most churches have endowments as do the national Christian organizations where they will invest the gift and just use the interest.

It's the kind of gift that can become a living memorial to your faith. We even get into some estates that can use trusts or life insurance to multiply a little of a family estate into a large donation." The attorney makes his final point on sharing the "final tithe" concept:

"This is just something I feel compelled to mention. We are a nation highly blessed and if everyone would give a little, the Lord's work would go on and on over the years. I've had couples who have left as much as half their estates and some who didn't leave any. But I'd feel bad if we never discussed the last gift you'll ever get to make."

Silence fills the room. The thought of mortality and making a faith statement moves beyond pieces of paper in a lawyer's office to a self-examination of faith, giving and death.

"I know this is something you will want to pray about. I am here as a scribe to draft what you want. But I can share with you that if we would use a paragraph like this in your Will, your kids would really understand the joy of your giving," he says.

The attorney hands out a sample faith statement with blanks to designate giving.

"Why don't you take this and think about it. I can insert it into the final draft. Or you might want to just leave a percentage to your choices. But think about this as an opportunity to both give and witness.

"And I need to remind you that I am not judgmental about what people give. This is your choice. I just feel it important to ask because most of the time this is something people just haven't discussed or thought about," the attorney adds.

"I had a couple who worked hard to build their small business, raise and educate their kids. They were always just a little short in giving to God during those years, so they decided to make up for some of their past poor giving by major gifts — half to a church endowment fund and half to the Christian college they attended. They also drafted their Wills to make some gifts to national Christian organizations that do a lot of things they believe in."

The attorney explains their Wills will come by mail in rough draft form so they can read them, jot down any questions, and check the accuracy. Then they are to make an appointment to come in to approve the final drafts.

The attorney also details the new federal requirements for health directives; discussing the differences between a durable power of attorney, a Living Will and some of the other options in estate planning.

The appointment ends with the attorney giving handouts to reinforce the things they have talked about during the appointment. The couple is invited to call if they have any specific questions.

Maria and Juan, and hundreds like them, leave with a new perspective on their estate. They have touched on and been provided answers for some of the most sensitive communication issues within their family and have obtained answers to questions that have lingered perhaps for years. They have been given the tools to make personal choices and an opportunity to make a faith statement within their Wills.

Has this been a life-changing day for Maria and Juan?

Only the Lord knows at this point.

God often leads us in His direction, a path formerly unseen and one we would never have followed.

"Where there is no vision, the people perish ..."

— Proverbs 29:18

walk in love

live in UNITY

YOU TAKE THE MEASURE OF INFLUENCE & IMPACT OF A TALL TREE ONLY AFTER IT HAS FALLEN.

HOW TO COMMUNICATE TO HEIRS THE JOY OF GIVING

"You have made known to me the path of life; you will fill me with joy in your presence, with eternal pleasures at your right hand."
— Psalm 16:11

CHAPTER 4

Just as communication between spouses can be a difficult area in estate planning, communication with children can be even more difficult. Why ruin a perfectly beautiful Sunday afternoon with a family meeting on estate planning? It just doesn't happen.

Yet most children are genuinely concerned about their parents' estate and have the best of intentions. They want to be sure Mom and Dad have enough money to live their golden years as well as possible. Because children can be called upon to "parent their parents" in health crisis situations, it is far better that all heirs know their parents' wishes and intentions.

An easy place to start is with a health

directive. This is a legal document outlining your wishes for medical treatment if you cannot make your health care decisions. Federal law requires that anyone entering a medical facility be presented written information from the facility on final health directive policies, which can be in the form of a Durable Power of Attorney or Living Will. The mechanics of those are detailed in Chapter Ten. Since they can have life or death consequences, a good starting point for thinking about and discussing estate planning is to make a decision on health directives in the event of a life-threatening illness. And it is far better to make those decisions during a time when a health crisis is not forcing the decision in a hospital emergency room.

... in health crisis situations, it is far better that all heirs know their parents' wishes and intentions.

A second way to ease into the issues of estate planning is to discuss the opportunities for giving by organ donation. The specifics of organ donation are provided in Chapter Eleven.

Thirdly, most people realize not all children grow up with the same set of values as their parents. Some children rebel. Others will become best friends of their parents. Some will live close by and others far away. Some will have frequent contact; others infrequent.

Parental instincts are to treat each child absolutely "equal" in distribution of their estate. In some cases, not treating each heir equally can lead to lifelong scars if children believe that by "winning the lucky gene bank" they are entitled to equal distribution with their siblings.

But there is nothing wrong with a Will that distributes estates based on other criteria, such as personal financial needs, the amount of parental support already given to a child, or other criteria. The vital communicative step is to specify by writing in a Will or trust the rationale for the distribution method chosen. It is important the heirs know why they are not treated equally.

How can heirs be kept from FIGHTING over Estates?

FAIR ISN'T
EQUAL,
AND
EQUAL
ISN'T FAIR

FAIR ISN'T EQUAL AND
EQUAL ISN'T FAIR
FAIR ISN'T EQUAL
AND EQUAL ISN'T FAIR

FAIR ISN'T EQUAL, AND EQUAL ISN'T FAIR

Money cannot buy love whether it is in the real world or through family estates. If one child needs greater support because of a disability, economic disparity or some other factor, parents should not hesitate stating that in their Wills and make their giving accordingly.

In other words, if a family has a multi-millionaire son and a daughter who stayed home to help take care of elderly parents, there is no written rule that says the estate has to be divided "equally." In fact, the multi-millionaire son may prefer any estate share be given to a trust for his heirs using favorable tax laws or accepting a lesser gift recognizing the need and financial contribution of his sister.

Jesus gave a wonderful message about the wayward son who squandered his estate and came back home in Luke 15:11-32:

> *Jesus continued: "There was a man who had two sons. The younger one said to his father, 'Father, give me my share of the estate.' So he divided his property between them.*
>
> *"Not long after that, the younger son got together all he had, set off for a distant country and there squandered his wealth in wild living. After he had spent everything, there was a severe famine in that whole country, and he began to be in need. So he went and hired himself out to a citizen of that country, who sent him to his fields to feed pigs. He longed to fill his stomach with the pods that the pigs were eating, but no one gave him anything.*
>
> *"When he came to his senses, he said, 'How many of my father's hired men have food to spare, and here I am starving to death! I will set out and go back to my father and say to him: Father, I have sinned against heaven and against you. I am no longer worthy to be called your son;*

make me like one of your hired men.' So he got up and went to his father.

"But while he was still a long way off, his father saw him and was filled with compassion for him; he ran to his son, threw his arms around him and kissed him.

"The son said to him, 'Father, I have sinned against heaven and against you. I am no longer worthy to be called your son.'

"But the father said to his servants, 'Quick! Bring the best robe and put it on him. Put a ring on his finger and sandals on his feet. Bring the fattened calf and kill it. Let's have a feast and celebrate. For this son of mine

was dead and is alive again; he was lost and is found.' So they began to celebrate.

"Meanwhile, the older son was in the field. When he came near the house, he heard music and dancing. So he called one of the servants and asked him what was going on. 'Your brother has come,' he replied, 'and your father has killed the fattened calf because he has him back safe and sound.'

"The older brother became angry and refused to go in. So his father went out and pleaded with him. But he answered his father, 'Look! All these years I've been slaving for you and never disobeyed your orders. Yet you never gave me even a young goat so I could celebrate with my friends. But when this son of yours who has squandered your property with prostitutes comes home, you kill the fattened calf for him!'

"'My son,' the father said, 'you are always with me, and everything I have is yours. But we had to celebrate and be glad, because this brother of yours was dead and is alive again; he was lost and is found.'"

In modern America, there are many prodigal sons and daughters. Estate planning can be an opportunity for restating family values and for healing sibling rivalries rather than reinforcing old hurts.

Just as everything we have is from God, everything in most estates given to siblings is from the use of the talents and the sacrifices of their parents. The entitlement to automatically get an equal sum is based usually on a parent's desire to not create hard feelings among siblings. In reality, hard feelings are created when siblings don't understand the thinking of Mom and Dad in allocating estate proceeds. Most children will accept, even though they may not like, a clear statement of giving to heirs if it is communicated to them properly.

Love Always

protects, trusts,
hopes, preserves.
Love never fails.

BLENDED FAMILIES ADD TO CONFUSION

With nearly 50 percent of marriages ending in divorce and remarriages, plus the growing numbers of additional marriages occurring after the death of a spouse, the problems of estate planning within "blended families" are even more complex.

This is an issue that should be settled when a widow, widower or divorcee remarries. And it can be done both in prenuptial agreements and in Wills. While some theological resistance exists to prenuptial agreements, because of state law which automatically can give a widow an "elective share" of an estate, it is important to the intentions of all parties to have a document spelling out the financial relationship of a blended family.

There is tremendous tension within a family if Mom dies and Dad remarries without addressing how family property is to be handled. And if this issue cannot be discussed and settled prior to a second marriage, it is a clue the marriage will have communication problems.

So what are the most effective ways for parents or children to communicate ideas concerning their estates?

1. In most families, visiting individually with each heir to discuss parental wishes is a good place to start. Very few families have "family meetings."
2. If there are objections or questions about a parent's plan, those should be discussed and resolved if possible.
3. Where special situations exist within families, those should be communicated to heirs verbally and within the estate-planning document.
4. By starting with goals and communicating these to the heirs, the decisions made by parents regarding their estates become much easier.
5. Children want to know their parents will be cared for so discussing life insurance, long-term care insurance, med-

ical coverage and other tools of elder law are equally important to a well-prepared estate plan.

One of the popular ideas with children and elderly persons is that they can somehow transfer all their property to their children and then be eligible for government funding of nursing home care. There is a serious theological question as to whether good stewardship exists when there is an attempt to circumvent the law by trying to get taxpayers to pay for care that could be paid out of accumulated assets. In other words, is it proper for families who have adequate resources to try to divert funds to obtain government funds for nursing home care? The law no longer allows this. Attempting to circumvent the law is really a form of stealing from others — taxpayers who don't have adequate resources and need the support of government programs. Recent federal laws provide for a "five year look back" rule to prevent transfer of assets for purposes of obtaining Medicaid nursing home care. It further provides criminal penalties for any attorney attempting to fraudulently draft such documents.

These laws refocus the need for every family to properly plan estates and utilize family assets giving parents their best care while still preserving estates. By law, the first use of family assets is for the care of parents who earned the money. In fact, some states make children legally responsible for their parents' care. God requires us to be care givers of our parents' needs.

> *"Give proper recognition to those widows who are really in need. But if a widow has children or grandchildren, these should learn first of all to put their religion into practice by caring for their own family and so repaying their parents and grandparents, for this is pleasing to God. . . . If anyone does not provide for his relatives, and especially for his immediate family, he has denied the faith and is worse than an unbeliever." — 1 Timothy 5:3-4, 8*

There are tools which can be used to keep family estates from being dissipated by illness. But it is critical these decisions be made as soon as possible because they generally involve forms of insurance. Nearly every insurance policy is cheaper when the decision to obtain it is made at the youngest age possible and when in optimum health. Every year those decisions are deferred, the greater the risk to families preserving estates and having adequate funds for Mom and Dad.

The greater our understanding of the tools to be good stewards of estates, the better chance families have to match their resources with their goals.

A Sampling of Various Hypothetical Clauses

A sampling of various hypothetical Will clauses illuminates how Wills can communicate various situations that can be helpful both in discussing family issues with heirs and, ultimately, how to express them in an estate plan. They are only discussion pieces and should not be used for final drafting of a Will.

To the family with a wealthy child and others making an average living:

"Love can never be measured in dollars. In making this Will, I express my love equally to all our children. But I also recognize the economic realities that each child is not equal. I recognize that David was able to get a medical degree and our family made sacrifices to help him obtain that. The other children could have done the same and we would have helped them. But we want to share our estate in a way that helps each child the most. Therefore, David's share of this estate equal to our other children shall be placed in a family trust. The funds shall be used for his children's education and, if unused, distributed equally amongst them when the youngest is age 30. The other children shall each obtain their share of my estate equally."

To the family with a disabled child: "Recognizing the special needs of Judy, it is our desire that her share of my estate shall be placed in a Hamilton Trust[4] for her benefit with the balance, if any, divided equally among our living children or their heirs upon her demise. The balance of my estate shall be divided equally among our children or, if they are deceased, their heirs at law shall be entitled to their share."

To the blended family with children from both spouses: "Recognizing I have remarried, I wish that my estate be placed in testamentary trust for the benefit of my spouse for life. Upon her demise, the balance shall be distributed equally to my children. Our property has been divided by title and in a prenuptial agreement so the ownership is clearly designated."

[4]A Hamilton Trust is a legal trust which, properly drafted, can allow a disabled child to continue receiving government benefits but provide access to the child's share of inheritance in the form of "life enhancement" funds as determined by the trust document and the trustee.

Illustration:
I wish all my bloodline to benefit from my good fortune. Recognizing this, I leave all of my estate to the John Doe Dynasty Trust™ to be used for the benefit of my existing and yet-to-be-known heirs.

To the family with an over-achieving child and a spendthrift or "troubled" child:

"Recognizing that John has succeeded beyond the expectations of the family and that Jason has in the past shown a reckless disregard for his possessions, I wish that my estate be divided equally between John and Jason. However, John's share shall be given to him outright and Jason's share shall be held in trust, receiving income only on an annual basis for his lifetime with the residual of the trust to his heirs *per stirpes*."

To the family with affluent children who don't "need" inheritance and parents wanting to leave everything to a charity, church or their grandchildren:

"Recognizing the successes all my children have accomplished in their lives, I wish that my estate be divided equally between the following organizations (list), my church, and all of my living grandchildren in trust."

To the family with a large net worth. Nothing is given outright but is placed in a Dynasty Trust™ for perpetual legacy:

"Leaving a legacy for future generations is of great importance to me. I wish all my bloodline to benefit from my good fortune. Recognizing this, I leave all of my estate to the John Doe Dynasty Trust™ to be used for the benefit of my existing and yet-to-be-known heirs."

Again, none of these clauses should be used in final form in drafting a Will. They are general illustrations to help in understanding how various situations in communicating with children can be handled. A detailed Will would be crafted to clearly communicate the intent of the Will to heirs.

A Faith Statement

Lastly, the opportunity of making a faith statement in a Will along with designating a "final tithe" is a tremendous opportunity. It serves several purposes:

1. Heirs clearly understand the value parents put on their giving to God.
2. Givers experience the joy of giving as good stewards to the work of Jesus Christ on earth that will continue years beyond their lives.
3. The church and its institutions can carry on their work and live the Gospel because they will have additional financial resources which might otherwise be directed to other spending in this age of consumption and consumerism.

Your Will Presents A Tremendous Opportunity to MAKE A FAITH STATEMENT To Accompany a Final Tithe.

A final gift in a Will can be done with a simple clause or a more formal faith statement. Consider three different types of faith statements that could become part of a Christian estate plan:

FAITH STATEMENTS

Three Examples:

Here I Stand:

"In making this Will, each of my children and heirs knows how important family is to me. No amount left in this Will can ever equal the love I have for each of you.

"But this is also a time to share a part of my blessings with God. I entered this world with nothing and I leave with nothing. I have tried to be a good steward of what God has given me. And with the joy of a cheerful giver, I want to leave a part of what has been given me to the work of the Lord with the following gifts: [Example]

____ percent of my estate to the endowment fund of ____(name)____ church.

____ percent of my estate to ____(name)____ college/university/seminary with the interest used for scholarships for students.

____ percent of my estate to the worldwide ministry ____(name)____.

"In making these gifts to the work of the Lord, I wish this to be a statement of faith asking my heirs to become cheerful givers of the talents and possessions given them so that generation after generation our family will be good stewards of what we have been given."

A Biblical Approach:

"In making this Will, I have considered the guidance given in the Bible on Christian giving. And while the gifts to each heir are important to me, so is this special giving to the work of Jesus Christ.

"Some of the verses that spoke to me include:

Include the Bible verses for your family to consider which you believe best give an eternal testimony to giving. Some of the verses in Chapter Two may be helpful.

"Therefore, before distribution to my heirs, I am making the following gifts to God's work in the spirit of these verses utilizing _____ percent of my estate as a "final tithe:"

_____ percent of my estate to the endowment fund of _____(name)_____ church.

_____ percent of my estate to _____(name)_____ Christian school/college/university/seminary with the interest used as scholarships for students.

_____ percent of my estate to the worldwide ministry of _____(name)_____.

The balance of my estate shall be divided equally amongst my three children or, if they are deceased, to their heirs *per stirpes*."

How can our Final Tithe bring glory to God?

Short and Simple:

"I believe each Christian should give part of his estate as a "final tithe" to the work of Jesus Christ. Therefore, I am making the following designations recognizing that all I have been given is from God and I want to share these blessings for his work.

"From my net estate after all expenses, taxes and other listed gifts, I hereby give _____ percent of my estate as a "final tithe" to be divided as follows:

_____ percent of my estate to the endowment fund of __(name)__ church.

_____ percent of my estate to __(name)__ college/university/seminary with the interest used for scholarships for students.

_____ percent of my estate to the worldwide ministry of __(name)__.

At the same time I leave to my family the rest of my estate as described in this Will."

THERE ARE MANY WAYS TO CRAFT YOUR ESTATE PROVISION

Of course, there are as many ways to word this provision as there are givers. It starts with writing your intentions and sharing your thoughts with your heirs, if that is your choice.

Whatever your decision, this is the final legal document you will prepare for your family and the world. It should reflect your values and your view of stewardship as well as your priorities for helping with the needs of this world.

Can you skip a "final tithe" and still go to heaven? Of course you can. The following verses can be instructive:

"For it is by grace you have been saved, through faith — and this not from yourselves, it is the gift of God — not by works, so that no one can boast." — Ephesians 2:8-9

"Jesus answered, 'I am the way and the truth and the life. No one comes to the Father except through me.'" — John 14:6

"... for all have sinned and fall short of the glory of God, and are justified freely by his grace, through the redemption that came by Christ Jesus. God presented him as a sacrifice of atonement, through faith in his blood. He did this to demonstrate his justice, because in his forbearance he had left the sins committed beforehand unpunished — he did it to demonstrate his justice at the present time, so as to be just and the one who justifies those who have faith in Jesus." — Romans 3:23-26

"No one who denies the Son has the Father; whoever acknowledges the Son has the Father also." — 1 John 2:23

There are many other verses which tell us the way. The ticket to heaven is not one that can be purchased with money. But the seriousness of our commitment to Christ's work can be incorporated into modern Christian Wills where a "final tithe" is our last opportunity to give a part of what we have been allowed to handle during our time on earth.

This decision should be made without a feeling of obligation but rather a sense of Christian joy that both God and family have shared in final choices.

Cheerfully Enter Into

the Joy of Giving!

You can take the measure of a tall tree only after it has fallen. This is what we discover when a great man or woman has died and we see the impact of their lives carried on in the lives of their family and those they influenced in the decades following their passing.

Last Will and
Will

HOW TO PREVENT FAMILY FIGHTS OVER ESTATES

Planning

"An inheritance quickly gained at the beginning will not be blessed at the end."
— Proverbs 20:21

CHAPTER 5

One major goal of parents considering Wills and estates is to avoid fighting among their children. In fact, that is a lifelong goal for most parents. Because parents love their children so much — even when at times they do not like their behavior — they will do virtually anything to preserve peace and tranquility among or between children.

Not unlike God's continual love for each person, parents love their children. "Love the sinner, hate the sin" can fit a lot of family relationships as well as God's relationship with us.

But just as Judgment Day has a finality for every life, the filing of a Will for dispersing a person's estate has an earthly finality. And the accountability and stewardship within that Will should be a concern to all believers.

Facing the Solomon-like task of being "fair to everyone" in Will planning requires nearly all of life's parenting skills. Some families handle this better than others.

Of course, if there is only one heir, the decision is much simpler — unless there is concern of a defecting spouse disputing an estate inheritance, an heir squandering the estate, creditors, or some other unforeseen attack on the heir's estate which could take much of what has been given. In that case, crafting a trust with "spendthrift"[5] provisions to prevent any unintended loss of a single heir's estate is strongly advised. Since there are legal ways to prevent an estate from being attacked by outsiders, even the parents with one heir wanting a "simple Will" should consider how "attack proof" they wish to make their heir's estate.

For parents with two or more heirs, the complexities and potential for conflict increase in geometric proportion to the number of heirs and their spouses. Even though spouses of heirs are seldom given part of an estate, they often have strong feelings whether the in-laws have treated their husband or wife fairly. Many families have adopted children. Sometimes natural-born children can have strong feelings about how adopted children are treated in estates. It is not infrequent these days for grandparents to be raising grandchildren and desire to treat them as equal to their children in estate distribution.

And the most complicated situations arise as more and more blended families inhabit Planet Earth because of the combined trends of divorce and longevity. Most divorcees remarry and the complications of "his" kids and "her" kids, which can even be combined with "our" kids, makes for interesting family relationships. Likewise, many older widows or widowers remarry, creating blended families. Sometimes their respective children are not thrilled that Mom or Dad

---

[5]These are legal clauses which can prevent a trust from attack by creditors, defecting spouses, or other claims.

remarried, and estates can become a tangible focus of unexpressed feelings about the remarriage.

These situations cry for high levels of communication about estate planning between the marital partners and families. Yet, just as high communication levels are needed, the trend is for little or no communication because of the complexities in attempting to be "fair to everyone."

Few family fights are over money, stocks, bonds, real estate or similar family assets if a Will is properly drafted. The division of these properties can usually be done according to a Will or trust distribution clause without a great deal of controversy. However, most "simple Wills" are written to divide real and personal property "equally among my heirs."

How Is Property Defined?

In accepting the lawyer's language in drafting this, very few clients distinguish between "personal property" and "personal effects;" the latter really requiring some definition.

The law of property is not hard to understand. Real property is the earth and all things affixed to it unless there is some written agreement to the contrary with the owner of property. Simply put, a carpet which is tacked down becomes part of "real property" and a loose carpet is "personal property."

So then what is "personal property?" It is everything else.

"Personal property" includes but is not limited to certificates of deposit, stocks, bonds, savings and checking accounts, cash, accounts receivable, promissory notes, tools, business equipment, cars, household goods, collectibles and collections, family heirlooms, rings, watches . . . Just think through the list of everything loose within your residence and in storage and you have defined your "personal property."

Confronted with this legal definition, most people want to distinguish between "personal property," which they generally want divided equally among heirs, and "personal effects," which are difficult to divide. As previously stated, how do you equally divide Mom's wedding ring between two daughters and Dad's shotgun between two sons? It is impossible. And it is the powder keg for sparking family feuds that never end. Even after the dissolution of a battle over "personal effects," the hurt, pain and feelings linger for a lifetime among siblings who feel they were not treated equally or fairly.

AVOID THOSE HORROR STORIES

There is hardly a family who does not have a horror story of a family member who in his opinion felt shortchanged in someone's estate. This animosity arises from three basic problems within family relationships:

1. Heirs develop false expectations about their entitlement because of a lack of communication by parents.
2. There is no way to divide some personal effects "equally."
3. And in most families sibling rivalries of the growing-up years, which may be suppressed for a time during adulthood, reappear in family estate fights just as they did when "the kids were kids."

There are some seasoned estate attorneys who can accurately predict the outcome of most sibling fights over personal effects by interviewing family members on how the kids fought while growing up. By determining who was the bully, who was the whiner, who was the peacemaker, who was content with whatever he got, who was the fighter, who had the feeling of being cheated, or whatever combination of these can be identified, the pattern of fighting in division of the personal effects or estates is highly predictable.

But the good news is there are ways to utilize a Will or trust provision to eliminate, or at least minimize family feuds over personal effects. To accomplish this, a legal definition of "personal property" and "personal effects" should be placed in the document.

By separating personal property and personal effects, the general assets of the estate can be divided equally or as the maker of a Will wishes and "personal effects" can be dealt with separately by another formula.

There are five major methods, with several combinations of each, used for dispersing personal effects in Wills or through trusts.

Personal Effects

... provided this shall not include my "personal effects" which are defined as:

> "Articles associated with person, as tangible property having more or less intimate relation to person or possessor."

Personal Property

"Personal property" can be defined as follows:

> "In broad and general sense, everything that is the subject of ownership, not coming under denomination of real estate. Generally, all property other than real estate."
>
> — *Black's Law Dictionary, Sixth Edition*, West.

DO NOTHING

First, parents can choose to do nothing. This is the most common alternative and needs to be highlighted in discussing this major family estate problem. Some parents make a conscious choice to do nothing. That is the way they resolved fights while parenting and that is their intention in estate planning.

"Just let the kids have it out. They'll work it out."

They will — with either the predictable outcome of the "sibling rivalry" formula of dispute resolution or in front of a judge who has to decide how to divide Aunt Maude's vase into thirds or Dad's shotgun in half.

Others unwittingly fall into the trap of "doing nothing" by failing to understand the legal difference between personal property and personal effects.

Since doing nothing or failing to properly define personal effects is the least satisfactory method of distribution to avoid family feuds, other options need to be considered.

RANDOM SELECTION

Secondly, the most popular method used by those who understand they can keep families from fighting is to establish within their Will a specific method for distribution. If distribution is by Trust, there needs to be a clear distribution clause in the Trust to give directions to the trustee. This is usually done by lot. The order in which heirs select items is also an issue and a personal choice.

Some family traditions would have the oldest to youngest pick in repeat order until all items are dispersed. Others would have all heirs draw a number and then pick in order until all items are dispersed. And some will have heirs draw numbers and pick first to last and then last to first in repeating order much like is done in games similar to "fantasy football." This has a tendency to equalize selections.

While random picking by heirs of personal effects is the most neutral of all systems, it does not recognize value. The person entitled to pick first may select the family Bible and the next person the piano. The third might pick a silver service setting. The outcome of using this method is the heirs make the choices and equality is achieved without parents playing favorites.

A general Will clause to carry out this random distribution method of personal effects could be similar to the following:

> *"I give, devise and bequeath all my personal effects to my children. Said property shall be divided through a process of random selection. The distribution shall proceed with my oldest living child selecting first and the remaining order of selection shall follow from oldest to youngest. When the youngest has made his/her first selection, the order shall be reversed for the next round of selection. This procedure shall continue until all property is distributed. Each child shall select one item with each pick. However, items that are in 'sets' or 'pairs' shall be considered 'one item' for purposes of this clause."*

Where can my final tithe have its greatest impact in proclaiming the word and witness of Jesus Christ?

Written List

A third method used by some families is using a written list of who gets what personal effects. Generally, heirs accept this even though they may not like the decisions because the intentions of parents are clear. This can be done by making a list and incorporating it as an exhibit within the Will. Using a clause similar to the following could allow utilization of this method of personal effect distribution:

> *"I give, devise and bequeath all my personal effects to my children to be divided equally between them except for the property specified in the attached Exhibit 'A'."*

Some parents will use a combination of specific designations plus the random selection method to dispose of their personal effects. This allows them to direct specific items to the heirs whom they feel would like to have special items and leave the rest of the items to random selection method. A Will clause to accomplish this combination method of distribution could be written in these terms:

> *"I give, devise and bequeath all my personal effects to my children to be divided as follows:*
> *1) My gun collection to my son Jim or his heirs at law;*
> *2) My golf clubs to my son William or his heirs at law;*
> *3) My family china set to my daughter Jennifer or her heirs at law.*
> *All of the rest of my personal effects shall be divided amongst my children through a process of random selection. The distribution shall proceed with my oldest living*

child selecting first and the remaining order of selection shall follow from oldest to youngest. When the youngest has made his/her first selection, the order shall be reversed for the next round of selections. This procedure shall continue until all property is distributed. Each child shall select one item with each pick. However, items that are in 'sets' or 'pairs' shall be considered 'one item' for purposes of this clause."

EQUAL VALUE DISTRIBUTION

A fourth method of distribution of personal effects which can be used is dividing personal property of approximately equal value into lots and then having the heirs draw for each lot. This method has worked well in big families with a large quantity of personal effects and when the heirs are primarily nieces and nephews. While it provides for a fairly quick and fair distribution of this property, it generally inspires the largest swap meet in the history of the family after each heir gets his lot. Amazingly, cousins who haven't spoken in years become nice to each other again as they trade a silver teapot for Uncle Jim's favorite rod and reel.

For those special situations where the donors believe the gifting by lot of personal effects is their best choice, the following type of Will clause can provide this method of distribution:

"I give, devise and bequeath all of my personal effects equally to my heirs at law. Said property shall be separated into lots of equal value by my Personal Representative with each lot numbered. Each heir shall draw an equal number of lots and that property shall be theirs. The heirs may exchange with others as they wish if they mutually agree, but none shall be obligated to do so."

AUCTION

The fifth method of distribution of personal effects is an auction. This can be a family auction or a public auction. Many consider an auction the fairest method of all. However, it doesn't always turn out that way. Families may have very wealthy siblings who have given little attention to their parents while pursuing careers in far off places, while other siblings may have stayed closer to their parents and have much more interaction with their parents and family heirlooms. Many times they have far less economic power than their wealthier siblings.

In either a public or private auction, the heirs having the most wealth have a tendency to end up with the more desirable family heirlooms. This can further accelerate feelings of disparity within a family.

This can be a very successful method of disbursement for some families, but the positive and negative aspects must be weighed. Also, many people have strong personal feelings about their personal effects and don't want the public "pawing through boxes" dividing the spoils of their lives.

If a private auction among the heirs is desired, the following Will clause could accomplish this:

> *"I give, devise and bequeath all of my personal effects to the care and custody of my Personal Representative. He shall coordinate a private auction amongst my children for the distribution of said property. Each child shall be given the opportunity to bid on any and all of said property at the auction. The proceeds from the auction shall be distributed to (charity, family trust, etc.)."*

And if a public auction of personal effects is desired, a Will clause along the following lines could accomplish this:

"I give, devise and bequeath all of my personal effects to the care and custody of my Personal Representative. She shall coordinate a public auction for the distribution of said property. All of my heirs shall be entitled to bid on any and all of said property at the auction. The proceeds from the auction shall be distributed to (charity, family trust, etc.)."

CREATIVE APPROACH

There is one other method that could be utilized. It is the method my wife and I personally chose after being professionally involved for over 30 years dealing with estate problems.

We created an irrevocable trust and placed all our "personal effects" and some "personal property" into the trust. We both have use of this property for our lives. Then the use, not ownership, passes to our children to use as long as they live. Then it is distributed to grandchildren by a formula we devised. This isolated all our "personal effects" from any attack by creditors, divorces or other claims — none of which we have experienced. But lawyers being trained to watch for all the "black clouds that roll out of the west" are sensitive to all the variables that could derail a carefully constructed estate plan.

The distribution clause used is as follows:

"Upon the demise of the last of Rollyn H. Samp or Karen A. Samp, the property shall be distributed equally amongst our children, or if any are deceased, their share shall go to their heirs per stirpes (the legal term for lineage by blood or adoption) *for their use for their natural lives except any item valued at less than One Hundred Dollars ($100.00) may be distributed by random selection, oldest to youngest, or sold by the trustee*

and proceeds divided equally amongst said beneficiaries if none of the beneficiaries wants them. All property shall be distributed by lot with each successor beneficiary picking a number and then selecting the balance of personal property in order until all property has been distributed for their lifetime use. Upon each of their demise, the property designated for their use shall be distributed to their heirs at law per stirpes and if they have none, said property shall be divided equally among the surviving heirs of Rollyn H. Samp and Karen A. Samp per stirpes by lot, provided any gifts given to us by any children or grandchildren shall be returned to them per stirpes."

ATTACK-PROOF WILLS

A frequent question is whether a Will can be made attack-proof by dissenting heirs. In most states it can be made attack-proof with an additional clause called an "incontestability clause." If this is lawful in your state, a variation of this clause should handle this problem:

"My Personal Representative herein appointed is hereby authorized to defend, at the expense of my estate, any contest or other attack on this document or any of the provisions herein stated. In the event that any beneficiary of this document shall singly, or in conjunction with any other person or persons, contest in any court the validity of this document or seeks otherwise to void, nullify, or set aside this document, or any provisions herein stated, the right of that person to take any interest given to him by this document shall be determined as it would have been determined had the person predeceased the execution of this document without surviving issue."

All of the provisions suggested in this chapter are for illustration purposes only. They should not be relied upon as legally enforceable in your state. They are offered as a guide for discussion between you and your personal attorney to craft a document that truly reflects YOUR WILL.

PRESERVING FAMILY BUSINESSES

Family businesses present special problems to prevent family feuds. These require an even greater sophistication in family communication and estate planning.

There are nearly 15 million family-owned-and-operated businesses in America today. It is predicted nearly half of these will pass from current owners to the next generation within five years. The U. S.

70% of family-owned businesses do not survive into the second generation

Chamber of Commerce found in a study that seven of ten family-owned businesses do not survive into the second generation.

Federal estate tax law regarding family businesses and family farms provide estate tax exemption of up to $1.35 million, designated to encourage families to keep family businesses.

The rules are complex and confusing, but here are the basics:

1. The decedent's interest in the business will qualify if 50 percent of the business is owned directly or indirectly by the decedent and members of the decedent's family, or 70 percent is owned by members of the two families, or 90 percent is owned by members of three families; **AND**
2. The decedent was a United States citizen or resident at the time of death; **AND**
3. More than 50 percent of the decedent's adjusted gross estate consists of business interests; **AND**
4. The business must pass to "qualified heirs," (i.e., spouse, lineal descendants, or even an "active employee" of the business who has worked at the business for at least ten years prior to the decedent's death); **AND**
5. The decedent, or members of the decedent's family, must have owned and materially participated in the business at least five of the eight years preceding the decedent's death; **AND**
6. The qualified heirs cannot sell or cease to materially participate in the business for a minimum of ten years following the decedent's death.

There are numerous ways family businesses can survive, but this generally requires a complicated estate plan.

The first critical element is whether family members are capable of running the business.

The second important area is whether the heirs can work together with siblings or in-laws.

And the third crucial decision is how to equalize an estate where one or two siblings are part of a going business and the others have left for their own careers.

Typical tools to minimize the problems in family-inherited businesses include:

- last to die life insurance to neutralize value for non-active siblings
- voting trusts with specific guidelines
- family partnerships with designated operating partners and a plan of succession
- Dynasty Trusts™ with clearly defined operational provisions
- or a combination of these and other very advanced estate-planning techniques

All of these require use of an estate professional who can work with a family to meet the goals of the founder and the objectives of those who inherit.

Happy are
those who
dream dreams
and are ready
to pay the
price to
make them
come true.

— L.J. Cardinal Suenens

"NOW FAITH IS BEING SURE OF WHAT WE HOPE FOR AND CERTAIN OF WHAT WE DO NOT SEE." — HEBREWS 11:1 — THE REALITY AND MAGNITUDE OF BELIEF AND THE WITNESS OF THE FAITH OF JESUS CHRIST AT WORK IN OUR LIVES IS IMMEASURABLE.

PRAY

USE THE PHONE

CALL LAW FIRMS

ASK QUESTIONS

FAITH

HOW TO GET AN ESTATE PLAN DONE

"By wisdom a house is built, and through understanding it is established; through knowledge its rooms are filled with rare and beautiful treasures."
— Proverbs 24:3-4

CHAPTER 6

The Chinese have a wonderful saying, "The best time to plant a tree was twenty years ago; the next best time is today." This is applicable to committing to an estate plan. Most of the tools to begin are in this book.

The first barrier to cross is a personal decision. If you believe it is good stewardship and good for your family to have an estate plan, then this is the time to put your decision into action.

If you have a spouse, this decision needs to be discussed and communicated. This is a difficult step. When the idea is first suggested, you might get a response like, "Are you sick or something?"

You might also face the typical stalling response of, "Yep, that's something we should do someday."

One technique might be to get your spouse to read this book. Or give your spouse a short outline of things you have learned from the book. Or highlight a few of the areas of the book that have been particularly meaningful or apply to you, your spouse or your family.

Many times a good way to get into the subject is by talking about problems you've been made aware of by others regarding their estates. Or find one of the many estate-planning seminars usually offered free of charge in your area and ask to attend those together. If these suggestions don't work, ask your spouse if it would be okay to accept a "free consultation" from an estate planning attorney and make an appointment.

And as previously suggested, discussing the need for a Durable Power of Attorney or Living Will, plus opportunities for organ donation, can be good ways to accelerate personal communication on the need for an estate plan.

In the meantime, try to gather articles or call for information which you can read and share with your spouse. Remember — fear of the unknown is a major barrier to taking any positive action in life. And the area of estate planning is fearful for most individuals.

The suggestion to make an appointment with a lawyer is a huge step toward completing an estate plan. Many people like "their" attorney but dislike the legal profession. This is largely because attorneys, by profession or obligation, take on many unpopular causes. And many of these become high-profile media events. If the legal profession is judged only by the public coverage of the O. J. Simpson trials and the various legal proceedings involving former President Clinton, very few people would want to talk to an attorney, except in an emergency.

But just as a few high-profile celebrities become symbols of their profession, lawyers should be judged individually — not by the unusual or sometimes bizarre cases which may stereotype them by the clients or causes they represent.

Most lawyers go to work every day doing their best to help people who cannot solve particular problems. If people could solve their problems themselves, they would not need to obtain an attorney. So the real business of "lawyering" is the profession of problem-solving.

I have the title "Counselor at Law" on my letterhead. I believe that fits best what I do. Most of the time I counsel clients about the law and how it can be used to solve a problem.

In recent years, legal advertising has become very popular. But picking an attorney based on his advertising in the phone book may not be the right way to find the attorney who can best represent you. In other words, the biggest ad may not belong to the best attorney.

One method of screening attorneys might be to contact the lawyers who are members of your church. You need to ask them three basic questions:

1. Do you or does someone in your firm handle estate planning?
2. If yes, about how many estate plans do you do a year?
3. If no, could you give me the names of three attorneys who are active in their churches and whom you believe would be good to see for an estate plan?

By asking these questions, you will obtain enough names to make an appointment. Just as you don't call the doctor for an appointment, don't call the attorney personally. You will get far more information in most cases by asking to speak with the attorney's personal secretary. You can tell the secretary you are thinking of completing an estate plan and want to know if the initial consultation with the attorney is free. If not, thank the secretary and hang up.

Hiring an attorney who may not fit your needs or give you the level of comfort you expect is not a good way to start an estate plan. You are going to discuss some of life's greatest "taboo" subjects with this person. You need to be as comfortable with your attorney as you are with your family doctor.

You should go ahead and meet with the attorney for an initial consultation. During the appointment your goal should be to determine whether this attorney understands your desire for a Christian-based estate plan, whether the attorney is organized to get the work done, can clearly explain answers to your questions and whether the attorney will put the estimated fees in writing. You are entitled to know these things before proceeding. If an attorney doesn't know the cost, ask to have the estimated fees put in a letter to you before scheduling a follow-up appointment. Most attorneys who are organized to handle estate work will be able to answer these questions without a problem. You will know what you are going to get, when you are going to get it, and how much it will cost. There should be no mystery to this and if a lawyer makes it sound mysterious or too complicated for you to understand, you may have ended up in the wrong office.

A major way to help the lawyer in developing your estate plan as simply as possible is to have all the initial information in writing. This will assist the lawyer and conserve time to discuss the estate rather than going over basic information.

Whatever Will or Living Trust you select, certain basic information is needed by an attorney to begin a discussion on your estate plan. The following questionnaire is a helpful guideline to prepare the basic information necessary to start working on an estate plan.

Legal forms can appear overwhelming … but this set, answered one question at a time, will lead you to a plan that fits your needs.

12. Do you have a Durable Power of Attorney? ❑ Yes ❑ No
Spouse? ❑ Yes ❑ No

13. Do you have a Living Will? ❑ Yes ❑ No
Spouse? ❑ Yes ❑ No

14. Do you have an Incapacitation Trust? ❑ Yes ❑ No
Spouse? ❑ Yes ❑ No

15. Do you have a Living Trust? ❑ Yes ❑ No
Spouse? ❑ Yes ❑ No

If you answered Yes to any of questions 11-15, please provide originals or copies.

16. Do you have minor children? ❑ Yes ❑ No
If no, please proceed to question 21.

17. In a joint demise of husband and wife, who would you like to raise your minor children?
First choice name and address:
Second choice name and address:

18. In a joint demise of husband and wife, it is recommended property be placed in trust for the minor children. Is this your wish? ❑ Yes ❑ No
If yes, who do you select as Trustee (the person who h… s)?
First choice name and address:
Second …

Estate Plan Questionnaire

Information provided is held in complete confidence and is used for the sole purpose of analyzing estate-planning needs and designing estate-planning documents.

1. Legal name:
Other names used:
2. Social Security Number:
3. Address:
4. Date of birth:
5. Phone number: (wk) (hm)
Spouse's Legal Name:
6. Other names used:
7. Social Security Number:
8. Address (if different from above):
9. Date of birth:
10. Legal names, addresses and birth dates of children:
11. Do you currently have a Will? ❑ Yes ❑ No
Spouse? ❑ Yes ❑ No

28. Do you wish to make a "faith statement" a part of your Will?
❑ Yes ❑ No

29. Other information — please provide the name and address of your:
CPA
Financial Advisor
Life Insurance Agent

30. Any questions you would like to dis… questionnaire.

… and principal of the trust to be …

… of the trust to be given to your children?

… ial trust may be

24. How do you want your personal property divided (if not received by your spouse)?
Options:
A. Lots
B. Let Personal Representative divide "equally"
C. Random selection
D. Designation of specific items written by you to be attached to Will
E. Auction
F. Other

25. Besides the specific bequests mentioned in question 23, how do you want the remainder of your estate distributed?

26. If your entire family meets a joint demise and all heirs are deceased, how do you want the estate distributed?

27. Whom do you want to administer your estate (Personal Representative)?
First choice name and address:
Second choice name and address:

Financial Information

Please fill out these sections as accurately as possible. Providing your attorney a complete financial statement allows him to fully evaluate and recommend an appropriate estate plan for his clients.

List all "major" assets (houses, cars, vacation homes, business interests, bank accounts, retirement accounts, CDs, real estate, stocks, bonds, life insurance policies, etc.), values, ownership interests (joint tenancy, tenants in common, individually owned), and beneficiaries (if applicable). Attach additional sheets if necessary).

Assets (What you own)	Estimated Value	How is Ownership Titled? (Husband, Wife, Joint, other)	Beneficiary

List all liabilities (car loans, mortgage, credit cards, etc.).

Liabilities (What you Owe)	Creditor	Name Loan Taken In (Husband, Wife, Joint, Other)	Amount Owed

ESTATE PLAN QUESTIONNAIRE

Information provided is held in complete confidence and is used for the sole purpose of analyzing estate-planning needs and designing estate-planning documents.

1. Legal name: ____________________
   Other names used: ____________________

2. Social Security Number: ____________________

3. Address:____________________
   ____

4. Date of birth: ____________________

5. Phone number:(wk)__________(hm)__________
   Spouse's Legal Name: __________

6. Other names used: ____________________

7. Social Security Number: ____________________

8. Address (if different from above):____________________
   ____

9. Date of birth: ____________________

10. Legal names, addresses and birth dates of children:
    ____
    ____
    ____
    ____

11. Do you currently have a Will? ❑ Yes ❑ No
    Spouse? ❑ Yes ❑ No

12. Do you have a Durable Power of Attorney? ❑ Yes ❑ No
    Spouse? ❑ Yes ❑ No

13. Do you have a Living Will? ❑ Yes ❑ No
    Spouse? ❑ Yes ❑ No

14. Do you have an Incapacitation Trust? ❑ Yes ❑ No
    Spouse? ❑ Yes ❑ No

15. Do you have a Living Trust? ❑ Yes ❑ No
    Spouse? ❑ Yes ❑ No

If you answered Yes to any of questions 11-15, please provide originals or copies.

16. Do you have minor children? ❑ Yes ❑ No
    If no, please proceed to question 21.

17. In a joint demise of husband and wife, whom would you like to raise your minor children?
    First choice name and address:
    ____
    ____
    Second choice name and address:
    ____
    ____

18. In a joint demise of husband and wife, it is recommended property be placed in trust for the minor children.
    Is this your wish? ❑ Yes ❑ No
    If yes, whom do you select as Trustee (the person who handles the funds)?
    First choice name and address:
    ____
    ____
    Second choice name and address:
    ____
    ____

If no, how do you want to dispose of this property?

____

____

____

19. While children are minors, how do you wish the income and principal of the trust to be used? (i.e., for their education, health, maintenance, etc.) ______________________

____

____

____

20. At what age would you like the balance of the trust to be given to your children? ______________________

21. Do you have handicapped or terminally ill children for whom a special trust may be necessary to protect their government benefits? ❑ Yes ❑ No
If yes, name(s) ______________________

____

____

22. What church or Christian organizations have been important to you or your family? ______________________

____

23. Are you interested in discussing a "final tithe" to your church or Christian organizations, colleges, ministries or memorials to charitable causes? ❑ Yes ❑ No
(List potential recipients for discussion.)

____

____

____

24. How do you want your personal property divided (if not received by your spouse)?
Options:
A. Drawing

B. Let Personal Representative divide "equally"
C. Random selection
D. Designation of specific items written by you to be attached to Will
E. Auction
F. Other

____
____
____
____

25. Besides the specific bequests mentioned in question 23, how do you want the remainder of your estate distributed?

____
____
____
____

26. If your entire family meets a joint demise and all heirs are deceased, how do you want the estate distributed?

____
____
____
____

27. Whom do you want to administer your estate (Personal Representative)?
First choice name and address:

____
____

Second choice name and address:

____
____

28. Do you wish to make a "faith statement" a part of your Will?
❑ Yes ❑ No

29. Other information — please provide the name and address of your:
CPA ______________________________
____
Financial Advisor ______________________________
____
Life Insurance Agent ______________________________
____

30. Any questions you would like to discuss not asked in this questionnaire.
____
____
____
____
____
____

FINANCIAL INFORMATION

Please fill out these sections as accurately as possible. Providing the attorney a complete financial statement allows him to fully evaluate and recommend an appropriate estate plan for his clients.

If the net value of your estate (assets less liabilities = net value) is over $1 million ($2 million for married couples), consideration needs to be given to a form of marital deduction Will with a credit shelter trust. We call it the No Tax Trust™. (They are called by many other names such as "A-B Trust," "Marital Deduction Trust," and others.)

List all "major" assets (houses, cars, vacation homes, business interests, bank accounts, retirement accounts, CDs, real estate, stocks, bonds, life insurance policies, etc.), values, ownership interests (joint tenancy, tenants in common, individually owned), and beneficiaries (if applicable). Attach additional sheets if necessary.

Assets (What you own)	**Estimated Value**	**How is Ownership Titled?** (Husband, Wife, Joint, other)	**Beneficiary**

List all liabilities.

Liabilities (What you Owe)	**Creditor**	**Name Loan Taken In** (Husband, Wife, Joint, Other)	**Amount Owed**

After completing the basic information which will help expedite your estate-planning, it is timely to consider whether you wish a "traditional will" or a "Spiritual Will."

A traditional will has in it all the necessary clauses and can include a "final tithe" as discussed previously. This is an acceptable choice in Christian estate planning. A "Spiritual Will" may be considered also. But a person is not a "better Christian" for picking a Spiritual Will over a traditional will. A sample of a traditional will with a "final tithe" and an incontestability clause to keep families from fighting over your personal effects follows:

I. Final Tithe

"Because we enter life with nothing and leave with nothing, I recognize that all that is in my estate is the result of God's blessings and not my work. While our family and their future is important, sharing with the work of Jesus Christ through the church and its organizations is an important part of my Last Will and Testament. Therefore, I give, devise and bequeath a final tithe to the following: (List) in the amount or percentage of my total net estates specified herein."

II. Incontestability (Legality to vary by state)

"My Personal Representative or any trustee herein appointed is hereby authorized to defend, at the expense of my estate, any contest or other attack on this document, any trust created herein or any of the provisions herein stated. In the event that any beneficiary of this document or any trust created herein shall, singly or in conjunction with any other person or persons, contest in any court the validity of this document or any trust created herein, or seeks otherwise to void, nullify, or set aside this document, any trust created herein or any provisions herein stated, the right of that person to take any interest given to him by this document, or any trust created herein shall be determined as it would have been

> *determined had the person predeceased the execution of this agreement without surviving issue."*

State law should be consulted prior to using a non-contest clause as they are not valid in all states.

III. The Spiritual Will

There has been a movement to resurrect the Spiritual Will which includes all the legal requirements of a traditional will but goes further in expressing a statement of faith for heirs to have for as long as they live. Spiritual Will clauses were utilized many years ago. A sampling is provided:

> *"In the name of God, Amen. I, Peter Cottrell of Prince William County Virginia being sick and weak in body, of sound and disposing mind and memory, knowing that it is appointed for all men to die, do make and ordain this my Last Will and Testament, commending my soul unto the hands of Almighty God, hoping alone for Salvation through the merits of Jesus Christ and my body to the dust to be buried in decent Christian burial at the discretion of my Executors. As to such Worldly Estate as it hath pleased God to bless me with I dispose hereof as follows . . ."*
>
> *Will of Peter Cottrell, 1803*

> *"In the name of God Amen. I, Peter Hush, of Rostraver Township in the County of Westmoreland and state of Pennsylvania being in a declining state of health of body but of sound and disposing mind, memory and understanding, considering the certainty of death and the uncertainty of the time thereof and being desirous of settling my worldly affairs and then may be the better*

prepared to leave this world when it shall please Almighty God to call me thence, I do therefore make and publish this my last will and testament in manner and form following that is to say . . ."

Will of Peter Hush, May 27, 1822

"In the Name of God. Amen. Be it known to all Men that I William Davidson yeoman and proprietor of Londonderry Inhabitant in the Village of Portapique in the District of Colchester Province of Nova Scotia, North America. Being weakly and sickly of Body but sound of Judgment and of perfect Memory being fully persuaded of the Certainty of my Death though uncertain as to the Time, after recommending my Soul to God and Committing my Body to the Dust in the Hope of a glorious Resurrection, For preventing all differences and Disputes after my Decease - Do Hereby appoint and Order my Temporal affairs as follows VIZ:"

Will of William Davidson, July 11, 1791

"In the name of God, Amen, the Twentieth Day of February, 1707-8. I, Paul Sears, Senr. of Yarmouth, in ye County of Barnstable, in New England, being at this time ill and weak in body but of Disposing mind and memory, Praised be God, Do make, Constitute, ordain and Declare this my Last Will and Testament, in manner and form following: First, and principally. I Comitt my soul to God, most humbly depending upon the gracious Death and merits of Jesus Christ my only Lord and Saviour for Salvation, and to the free pardon of all my sins. And my Body to the Earth to be buryed in such Decent Christian manner as to my Executors hereafter named shall be thought fitt. And as for my outward

Estate, as Lands, Chattels and Goods, I do order Give and Dispose in manner and form following:"

Will of Paul Sears, 1707

"In the name of God Amen. I William Beadles of said State and County being of advanced age and knowing that must shortly depart this life, deem it right and proper both as respects my family and myself that I should make a disposition of the property which a kind providence has blessed me with; do therefore make this my last Will and Testament, hereby revoking all others heretofore made by me; My Soul I trust shall return to rest with God who gave it as I hope Eternal Salvation through the merits and atonements of the blessed Savior Jesus Christ whose religion I profess:"

Will of William Beadles, July 1866

The Spiritual Will Project, headed by Atlanta attorney Tim Minor[6], encourages Christians to consider Spiritual Wills.

Spiritual Wills are simply standard Wills with one or more spiritual messages included. It offers you an opportunity to make an eternal "last testament" about your faith in God, your love for Jesus, forgiveness and your prayer for the future. Since it is read after your death, it can be a powerful way to offer inspiration and comfort for your family. And through your Will, they may come to know Jesus. They certainly know forever what you believed.

A Spiritual Will permits you to:

- make a statement to your family about your belief in God and faith in the everlasting salvation;
- offer your family comfort, love and forgiveness that will help them overcome the difficult period after your death;

[6]Tim Minor, Attorney at Law, Spiritual Will Project, 540 Powder Springs Street, Marietta, Georgia.

- remind them of your source of strength in a troubled time and give them encouragement for the future; and
- continue to make spiritual statements to generations of your family to come.

A Spiritual Will is enforceable by the courts and is as flexible as the maker wishes it to be. The spiritual message contained in the Will gives it power and everlasting force.

A sample of a Spiritual Will using the same basic legal premise of a traditional Will is provided as a sample:

> "In the name of God, Amen. I, ______________________, of (address) ______________________ express in my Last Will and Testament as described herein my thankfulness for each day God has given me on earth. I am humbly grateful for the many talents and blessings given me that have allowed me to be a witness for Christ each day even though as a sinner I have failed. You should all take comfort in knowing that I am now with the Lord as you read my Final Will and have exchanged my earthly possessions for eternal life. I ask forgiveness for all sins I have failed to communicate and ask those who have hurts and harm to forgive each other. It is these possessions I pass to those named and ask that you accept them as gifts from the Lord rather than gifts from me. We are born with nothing and leave with nothing, so these gifts are merely those which God allowed me to have as His steward while on earth. You can do what you wish with these gifts just as God gives us all freedom to choose. But the right choice is to use these to honor the Lord in all that you do. Shed only tears of joy for even though I am physically not with you, just as Jesus physically left this earth, for those of you who believe and are faithful, we will be reunited in the eternal home He has prepared for us. To those of you who choose not to follow this path, my final prayer is for your conversion that you may be spared eternal damnation." (The balance of the Will outlines all gifting and other provisions as a regular Will.)

Procedure for Will Drafting

When you go to a lawyer for a Will, the attorney conducts an in-depth interview about your property, family and wishes. The attorney then drafts the Will by first assembling standard Will provisions. These clauses are then adapted to the individual situation. The Will is then prepared for signature.

If you desire a Spiritual Will, the same process is used. However, additional clauses are added regarding faith, love and hope as desired. These provisions can be drafted and requested to be included in the Will. It's just that simple. One can use the samples provided or simply write your own.

Whatever your choice, the decision is yours. You can pick what you believe best reflects how you wish the last legal document anyone may read from you will be communicated.

"The best time to plant a tree was twenty years ago; the next best time is today."

Chinese Proverb

A message on the importance of planning ahead & remembering those you cherish.

Treasured Memories

WHY SHOULD YOUNG PARENTS HAVE A WILL?

Your Will

"A good man leaves an inheritance for his children's children . . ."
— Proverbs 13:22

CHAPTER 7

There is a frighteningly large percentage of young parents who do not have Wills. Yet for the sake of their minor children, those parents need wills the most. Young parents typically do not feel the need to make a Will because they generally do not have large estates and may consider estate planning as something for older, wealthier people. However, in the event of the joint demise of young parents, the issue of who raises their children and how their funds are handled becomes a monumental family question. Frequently, children of parents who have both been killed end up with fairly large estates due to wrongful death claims or life insurance proceeds. These factors are usually not considered by young families until the issues of handling these funds are explained to them.

In addition to the assumption that only older people need estate planning, there is a good deal of resistance to drafting Wills by young couples because they simply cannot agree on who should raise their children if something should happen to them. Again, communication becomes a potential barrier in addressing possible estate problems.

I want to leave my family in a financial position to continue living as if I were still alive.

There are three principal issues needing to be addressed by young families in estate planning:

First, if both parents are deceased, who should the courts appoint to serve as the legal guardian over the children? If there is no Will, this can lead to a lengthy legal proceeding wherein the courts may conduct a home study to determine who would be the best person to raise the minor children. Because there is no Will, it is difficult to determine the desires of the parents. However, if there is a Will nominating a guardian, the courts will generally appoint that person guardian unless there is evidence showing the person nominated to be unfit, incompetent, or for some other reason physically unable to raise the children.

The subject of who would be best to raise the children if the parents are gone requires a good deal of discussion and has potential conflict as described in the "Pyramid of Risks."

It is acceptable in naming guardians to have successor guardians in the event the first named parties cannot serve. For

Young Family Questions

Who will raise the kids if both of us are killed in an accident?

How much life insurance is needed if my spouse or I die, to support the kids?

How do I talk to my parents about their estate?

Should I have a trust for the kids if something happens to us, so they don't squander the money?

If I die and my spouse remarries, could the new spouse spend my life insurance?

At what age should children be given money from a trust?

Who should be the children's guardian if we both die?

example, many families will select one of the grandparents to raise the children, but if they are gone or incapacitated a successor person is pre-named in the Will, such as a sister, brother, brother-in-law or sister-in-law, who could fulfill the role of a guardian.

Secondly, a decision on young-family Wills must be made regarding who should supervise any money belonging to the children. Because children can have substantial sums of money through inheritance, wrongful death recoveries, or life insurance proceeds, a conservator over the property of the children is also recommended and can be legally required.

The guardian and conservator can be the same person. These titles change from state to state depending on state law. In general, a guardian is someone who is legally in charge of the person while a conservator is someone who is legally in charge of the money.

The decision and discussion on whether the guardian and conservator should be the same person has to do with parenting. Many times it is difficult for a guardian to obtain appropriate discipline over children if they also have control of the money. Many times families will appoint a guardian over the children and then appoint the guardian as a co-conservator with another party so there is a check and balance.

Thirdly, there is a question of how to finance raising children if something happens to both parents. This is most frequently done with life insurance providing a sum adequate to raise the children in the manner the parents would have raised them.

Much of the legal hassle can be eliminated by appropriate clauses within a Will. This can be done in the form of a testamentary trust. A sample is provided for general guidance to illustrate this:

IN CASE OF A JOINT DEMISE

"In the event my wife, __(name)__ precedes me in death, I give, devise, and bequeath to __(names of Trustees)__, in trust for the benefit and use of my children for their support, maintenance, and education, all the rest and residue and remainder of my estate, both real and personal, providing:

A) The said trustees take possession, hold, manage, invest, and reinvest the proceeds of the trust and collect income therefrom and use the balance of the income, together with any part of the corpus that is necessary, in their sole and absolute discretion for the support, maintenance, and education of the beneficiaries.

B) I hereby authorize and empower the trustees to hold and continue in their discretion any securities in which any of my property may be found invested at the time of my death and they shall not be liable for any shrinkage in value by reason of the exercise of the discretion hereby reposed in them. I further hereby authorize and empower the trustees herein named in their discretion to sell and dispose of any and all of my property, real and personal, either at public or private sale, and at such time or times and upon such terms as they believe proper, and to give to the purchaser of said property all deeds, bills of sale, assignments, or other instruments of title as may be proper.

C) That upon my youngest child arriving at the age of 21 years, said trust shall terminate and the balance of the trust, together with any and all accumulations, if any, should be distributed to my children equally, and if any are deceased prior to that time, their heirs at law shall take by right of representation.

If for any reason __(names of Trustees)__ are unable to serve as trustees, then in that event I give, devise, and bequeath to __(names of successor Trustees)__, in trust for the benefit and use of my children for their support, maintenance, and education, all the rest and residue and remainder of my estate, both real and personal, subject to the same provisions and rights and restrictions as above mentioned.

If my wife dies prior to my death, and any children born of our marriage are under the age of majority, and it is necessary that a guardian be appointed, it is my wish and desire that __(names of guardians)__ be appointed as guardians of said minors. If for any reason they are unable to serve as guardians, then in that event it is my wish and desire that __(names of successor guardians)__ be appointed as guardians of said minors."

Today I'm
Celebrating
My Birthday

NOTES FOR MY WILL:

Leaving Jennifer, Katie
and Beca... & friends

Our life insurance?
Health coverage?
Mutual Fund status?
Remind them to share
my video tape with
special friends.
Support Food for the
hungry!
Include a Final Tithe
in our plans...
Celebrate where I am
going to be for
Eternity and be
thankful for my
good life.
— Chris

dreams
A Book of Symbols

He is
Risen.

VALID THIS DATE ONLY
2142811
DAILY PARKING PERMIT
Those who have passed from this world really die only when we, whom they loved, choose to forget them.
(A will is a way to be sure you are not forgotten.)
Will
Dad Thanks for Taking the Time

There are numerous other clauses to accomplish the parents' desires. The most important step is the necessity for parents to think about these three key questions that need to be answered in the event a tragedy would happen within their family, leaving their children without their natural parents.

"Life is not a dress rehearsal.
This is the real thing.
We make choices that have
consequences for a lifetime."

Mike Huckabee, "Living Beyond Your Lifetime"

PROTECTION

LIFE INSURANCE

Last Will and Testament

"Estate planning is about identifying financial goals and objectives, then implementing them in a comprehensive legal plan."

— ROLLYN H. SAMP

HOW TO USE LIFE INSURANCE AS A TOOL IN ESTATE PLANNING

"Where there are no oxen, the manger is empty, but from the strength of an ox comes an abundant harvest."
— Proverbs 14:4

CHAPTER 8

Estate planning is about identifying financial goals and objectives, then implementing them in a comprehensive plan. Identifying goals and objectives is a personal process which should be thoroughly discussed with your spouse and family. Once a decision has been reached on what type of legacy is to be left, an attorney and other financial-planning professionals should be consulted to provide you with various estate-planning options.

Estate plans are like people; each unique in its own way. The components of an estate plan can vary significantly — from a widow needing nothing more than a simple

Will to accomplish the disposal of property to heirs upon her demise to a husband and wife needing various trusts and more complicated Wills to satisfy their final objectives. Although not all estate plans are alike, certain estate-planning tools should be considered for each plan. A few of the more obvious tools are Wills, living trusts and durable powers of attorney. Yet another obvious option — but nonetheless often overlooked — is the use of life insurance as part of a well-crafted estate plan.

WHY LIFE INSURANCE?

People are sometimes skeptical about life insurance and life insurance agents because it is a sales-driven product with agents aggressively marketing the benefits. Furthermore, the realization that "I'll pay money into a policy all my life and it won't do me any good because nothing is realized until I'm dead" is unsettling and unmotivating. People holding this opinion fail to realize that when correctly used, life insurance is an invaluable estate-planning tool that can provide cash to heirs free of federal estate taxes. There are hundreds of life insurance products which can enhance both personal financial plans and estate planning.

Life insurance is one of the few remaining estate-planning tools which allows for generational transfer of wealth without incurring estate taxes or probate fees if properly owned. It will remain an important tool until the federal estate tax is completely repealed. If two of your estate plan goals are to avoid federal estate taxes and provide liquidity for your heirs, life insurance should be considered.

However, if not structured correctly, proceeds from a life insurance policy can be taxed in estates. If your taxable estate is at or exceeds the applicable exclusion amount, it is important to take steps to keep the proceeds out of your taxable estate. Proceeds from a life insurance policy can be included in your estate if any of the following apply:

1. If the proceeds are payable to or for the benefit of the insured's estate; or
2. If the insured had any "incidents of ownership" in the policy when she died (i.e., right to change beneficiaries, right to borrow against the policy); or
3. The insured transferred ownership rights in the policy to another person or a legal entity within three years of death.

Just because your policy meets one of the three conditions above does not mean your situation cannot be changed. Policies can be gifted to heirs or to irrevocable life insurance trusts which legally remove "incidents of ownership." You can also change your policy beneficiary designation to take advantage of any new tax laws.

... if not structured correctly, proceeds from a life insurance policy can be taxed in estates.

There are two fundamental goals of estate planning: avoiding taxes and distributing assets to those you select. Unfortunately, not every estate plan eliminates all estate taxes. In these cases, life insurance can provide the cash necessary to cover estate taxes, leaving your entire estate to heirs as intended.

This exemption is eliminated in 2004 when the personal exemption amount increases to $1.5 million. In addition to the applicable exclusion amount $1,000,000 in 2002 and gradually increasing, an estate can claim an additional federal estate tax exemption for qualifying family-owned businesses. The rules are complex and confusing, but here are the basics:

For business owners, life insurance can allow for the passage of the business to an intended heir while providing cash to other heirs. For example: George owns a small business worth $1 million. He is a widower and has two children, Chris and Mary Kay. Chris helps George in the family business and wants to continue in the family business after George dies. Mary Kay lives in the city and has no desire to own part of the family business. George has spoken to Chris and Mary Kay and understands their feelings. George wants to treat Chris and Mary Kay equally, but he also wants Chris to own the entire business outright. To alleviate this problem, George has Mary Kay purchase a life insurance policy on his life. Mary Kay is the owner and beneficiary of the policy. George gifts the money to Mary Kay to pay for the premiums (George can legally gift up to $10,000 to Mary Kay per year tax free). George executes a simple Will leaving everything to Chris. When George dies, the business is left to Chris and the proceeds of the life insurance policy are paid to Mary Kay. George has achieved his goal of leaving the business to Chris. And he has made both children financially equal by purchasing life insurance. Additionally, with the life insurance policy, George increased the amount transferred to Chris and Mary Kay from $1 million to $2 million without incurring federal estate taxes.

> Life insurance can also be an important tool to achieve "final tithe" goals ...

This is only one simple example of using life insurance to solve a family estate problem. There are numerous types of life insurance; varieties of term, universal, whole life and variable life. Most

life insurance agents have concentrated training and experience in the use of life insurance for estate planning.

Getting competitive presentations from life insurance agents can be very educational in making the right choice on this key estate-planning tool. Life insurance can also be an important tool to achieve "final tithe" goals because of its flexibility and unique financial/legal characteristics.

Here are some examples of proper uses of life insurance in an estate plan: [**CAUTION:** ***Because of the new estate tax laws and potential for changing or even repeal, these are only illustrations and should not be relied upon for estate planning. They are meant to help develop questions and ideas in preparation for estate planning discussions with your life insurance agent and/or attorney or other professional in estate planning.***]

A widow with two children and an estate worth $2 million.

Estate taxes without life insurance to supplement in 2002-2003.

$2,000,000	estate
1,000,000	federal exemption from estate tax*
$1,000,000	subject to federal estate taxes (Estate taxes on a $1,000,000 taxable estate equal approximately $435,000.)

$1,000,000	taxable
-$435,000	federal tax
$1,565,000	out of $2 million remains for two children

*Note the exemption changes through 2010 (see Chapter 12)

Assume the same as above, except the two children own a $500,000 policy on their mother's life. The taxable estate would remain the same. However, the $500,000 from the insurance policy would be used by the heirs to pay the $435,000 federal estate tax bill.

Estate Taxes with Life Insurance Supplement.

$1,000,000	taxable estate
-$435,000	federal estate taxes
$565,000	remaining
+$500,000	proceeds from life insurance
$1,065,000	
+$1,000,000	federal exemption from estate tax
$2,065,000	for her heirs (less the premiums paid for life insurance)

GIFTING

Life insurance also remains, under the new law, an important gifting tool because outright lifetime gifts of over $1 million will be taxed at the prevailing gift tax rate. After 2010, the $1 million lifetime gift will be indexed for inflation and all sums given above that amount to individuals will be taxed at 35 percent. Of course, gifts to religious organizations and charities remain tax free under federal law.

PROTECTING LIFE INSURANCE TAX-FREE STATUS

While properly purchasing and titling life insurance as well as naming beneficiaries can be a complex area when trying to legally avoid federal estate taxes, there are three general ways to prevent inclusion of life insurance proceeds in an individual's taxable estate:

To accomplish this, life insurance proceeds cannot be payable to your estate. If you name your estate as beneficiary of your life insurance policy, the proceeds will be included in your taxable estate. Therefore, the beneficiary(ies) of your life insurance policies need to be someone other than "the estate." In other words, it needs to be in the name of individuals or trusts intended to receive the money.

Secondly, even if you do not name your estate as beneficiary of your life insurance policy, the proceeds can still be included in your taxable estate if you had any incident of ownership in the policy at your death. Examples of "incident of ownership" include: the right to change beneficiaries, the right to surrender the policy, or the right to borrow against the policy.

Thirdly, the proceeds of your life insurance policy can be included in your taxable estate if you transfer ownership of the policy to someone else within three years of death.

However, as with other assets, life insurance proceeds are not included in your taxable estate if the beneficiary is your spouse because of the unlimited marital deduction. The unlimited marital deduction allows for unlimited transfer of assets between husband and wife during life and at death without taxation consequences.

While this is a very general discussion of life insurance uses, this is an area where having goals clearly outlined and having the assistance of a person knowledgeable in the use of life insurance for estate planning is invaluable.

These are just three general areas of caution to show how improper planning can lead to unnecessary taxation. None of these examples should discourage a discussion on the use of life insurance in estate planning. There are many ways to assist estate-planning through its use, though it must be tailored to each person's needs, desires and financial capabilities.

LIFE INSURANCE FLEXIBILITY

Life insurance has been a dynamic and ever-changing business devising new products to help in estate planning and personal finance. The use of annuities, last-to-die policies, and new term policies which do not mature or endow at age 100, are just a few examples of new products.

The key to utilizing life insurance

as a valuable tool of estate planning is having a life insurance agent working with your estate planning attorney who clearly understands your financial situation, estate planning goals, and the necessary resources to implement them.

AN ATTORNEY EXPERIENCED IN ESTATE PLANNING CAN CRAFT A TRUST TO FULFILL YOUR GOALS JUST LIKE AN ARCHITECT CAN TAKE YOUR IDEAS FOR A HOUSE AND DRAFT A PLAN TO CONSTRUCT YOUR DREAM HOME.

—Rollyn H. Samp

WHAT ABOUT TRUSTS, LIFE ESTATES AND JOINT TENANCY?

TRUSTS
Life Estates and Joint Tenancy

"He who fears the Lord has a secure fortress, and for his children it will be a refuge."
— *Proverbs 14:26*

CHAPTER 9

There are as many combinations of trusts as there are specific needs for each estate. Many times people think of bank-administered trusts when the word is mentioned. However, many trusts are stand-by trusts that may be used in only special situations and there are family-administered trusts.

Four simplified definitions can be helpful in understanding the basics of trusts:

Trusts: *Legal documents creating an entity to carry out specific actions as decided by the Trustor.*

Trustor: *Also called Grantor or*

Benefactor. The person(s) who makes the Trust and transfers property into it.

Trustee: *The person(s) or institutions managing the Trust by the terms and conditions in the Trust document.*

Beneficiaries: *Those who receive distributions on benefits from the Trust as outlined in the Trust document.*

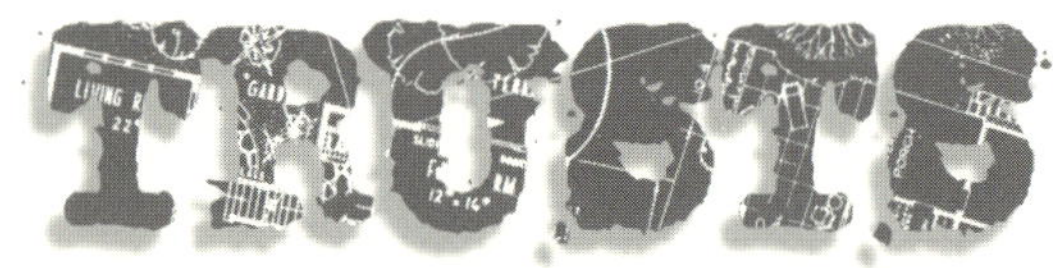

Trusts are a very useful tool which range from a "young family trust" outlined in a Will to provide care for minor children in the event of the parents' joint demise, to complicated Dynasty Trusts™ for families wanting to preserve their family wealth for generation after generation in perpetuity.

The best way to decide whether or not you need a trust is to outline for an attorney the goals you wish to accomplish and ask if a trust would be helpful. Just a few of these goals might be:

- taking care of minor children if both parents die at the same time;
- taking care of an elderly person who cannot handle his affairs;
- establishing funds for grandchildren;
- establishing a trust to restrict children from "wasting" their inheritance;
- keeping life insurance from creating a potential tax liability.

The following list of popular trusts and how they are used

gives a snapshot of the great variety of tools available to a competent estate planner if your wishes are clearly communicated.

Revocable Living Trust — Created and funded during a trustor's lifetime. It is intended to reduce probate and other administrative costs associated with post-death estate work. The trustor generally acts as trustee and retains control over trust property until death.

Testamentary Trust — A trust created at death, usually through a Will. It is generally designed to hold property for minors, disabled beneficiaries or until an heir reaches a specific age.

Charitable Remainder Trust (CRT) — A Charitable Remainder Trust is an excellent estate planning tool for someone desiring to donate assets to a charitable organization but still retain an income interest.

A simple explanation of how a CRT works is as follows: A trustor (donor) irrevocably gifts property into the CRT. The trustee manages the property for the duration of the CRT, which is either a specified number of years or for the trustor's life. The trustor receives income from the trust for as long as the CRT exists. When the trust terminates, the assets of the trust are left to one or more charitable institutions as named beneficiaries.

There are definite advantages in creating a CRT, namely that contributions and distributions can qualify for income and estate tax deductions. You should consult an estate planning attorney to determine if a CRT is right for you.

Irrevocable Life Insurance Trust — A trust designed to own a life insurance policy on the life of the trustor. It is used to pass death proceeds from the policy to heirs without inclusion of proceeds in the trustor's taxable estate.

Charitable Remainder Annuity Trust (CRAT) — Trust whereby the beneficiary receives a fixed dollar annuity at least annually for life. When the trust terminates, usually on the death of the trustor, the remainder of the trust passes to charity. It is designed to utilize the estate tax charitable deduction.

Charitable Remainder Unitrust (CRUT) — Same form as CRAT except the beneficiary receives an amount for life based on a fixed percentage of the fair market value of trust assets.

To fulfill your goals, you can craft a Trust.

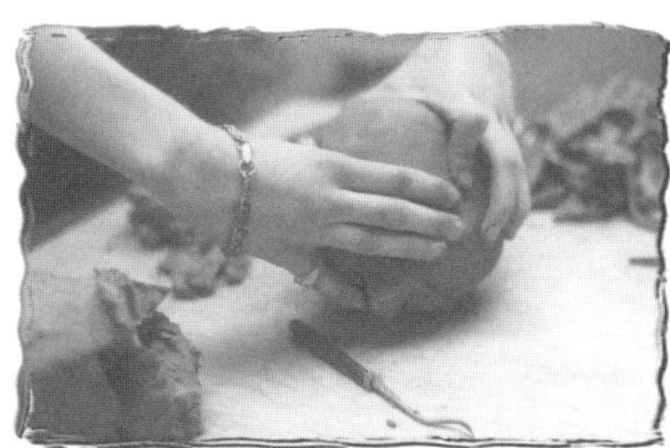

Minors ss2503(c) Trust — Trust designed to hold property for minors and to qualify for the gift tax annual exclusion. Trust income is accumulated in the trust until a minor reaches age 21. When the minor reaches 21, the principal and income pass directly to him.

Minors ss2503(b) Trust — Same as above except income from the trust is distributed to the minor prior to age 21.

Charitable Lead Trust — A split-interest trust. Similar to a CRAT or CRUT. The estate owner makes a charitable contribution to the annuity interest for income tax deduction purposes. But a reversionary interest in the trust's corpus (legal jargon for "the principal") is retained by the estate owner for himself or his family.

Grantor Retained Income Trust (GRIT) or Qualified Personal Residence Trust (QPRT) — Device used to transfer the personal residence of the trustor to heirs at a discounted basis while the trustor retains the right to live in the residence for the length of the trust. At the termination of the trust, the title to the residence passes to the heirs.

Grantor Retained Annuity Trust (GRAT) — Device used to transfer assets to heirs at a discounted basis while the trustor receives an annuity (based on a fixed rate of return and based on the assets transferred to the trust) for the length of the trust. When the GRAT terminates, the assets pass to trustor's heirs.

Grantor Retained Unitrust (GRUT) — Same as GRAT except the annuity for the trustor is readjusted annually and is structured upon a fixed rate of return on the fair market value of the trust assets.

Generation Skipping Trust — Trust used to pass assets from one generation to another generation at least two generations removed; i.e., from grandfather to granddaughter. It is generally designed to utilize a person's $1,000,000 Generation-Skipping Transfer Tax exemption. Created either during a person's lifetime or by Will.

Dynasty Trust™ — An irrevocable trust established to benefit numerous generations and designed to exist as long as allowed by applicable law. It is created either during person's lifetime or at death.

Reverse Qualified Terminable Interest Property (QTIP) Trust — Created at death, usually through a Will. It is a trust qualifying for the unlimited marital deduction whereby the surviving spouse receives income for life. But the original decedent is considered the transferor for Generation-Skipping Transfer Tax purposes.

There are as many varieties of Trusts as there are those who make them.

Qualified Terminable Interest Property (QTIP) Trust — Created at death, usually through a Will. Used for the benefit of a surviving spouse and designed to qualify for the unlimited marital tax deduction. The surviving spouse receives income

for life from the trust and can invade the principal if necessary. Assets from the trust are included in the surviving spouse's estate upon death.

Qualified Domestic Trust (QDOT) — Special form of QTIP trust for a non-citizen spouse. QDOT is needed to take advantage of the unlimited marital deduction. The marital deduction is not allowed for a non-citizen spouse unless assets are placed into a QDOT.

Credit Shelter Trust — Also known as a Bypass Trust, A-B Trust, Marital Deduction Trust, or No Tax Trust™. Created at death, usually through a Will. It is designed to contain an amount equal to a decedent's applicable exclusion trust. The purpose is to maximize a decedent's federal estate tax exemption. Assets in the trust are not included in the surviving spouse's estate and pass to heirs' estate, tax free upon termination of the trust.

Asset Protection Trust — Trust usually established outside of the United States. It is designed to make a creditor's claims against the trust more difficult to enforce. A foreign trustee is generally given complete discretionary authority relating to income and principal distributions to the trustor.

Rabbi Trust — Trust created by an employer for an employee's benefit. It is generally used for deferred compensation contracts and funded with a life insurance policy.

Spendthrift Trust — Created to provide protection for the principal and income of the trust from a beneficiary's creditors. Neither the principal nor the income of the trust can be liable for the debts of any beneficiary and no beneficiary can have any power to sell, assign, transfer, encumber or dispose of his interest in the trust or the income produced thereby prior to the actual distribution.

With this brief summary of trusts, it is obvious when wishing to craft a trust that professional advice be utilized. Basically, an attorney can draft a trust to meet the communicated desires and goals of any family. The difficulty is in clearly identifying those goals, contemplating future situations, and then drafting the language to match those intentions.

JOINT TENANCY

Putting property in joint names between spouses or children is many times substituted for estate planning. People think this is a cheap and effective way to plan their estates. However, this is not true. Joint tenancy can cause problems with larger estates in loss of the marital deduction for federal estate taxes. In states having inheritance tax, this is usually attributable to the owner of the funds and can lead to family feuds over the intentions of the parties in distributing property.

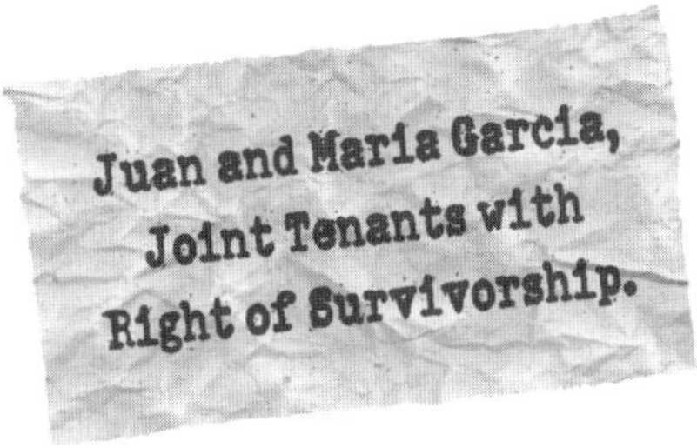

Except where a state law provides an "elective share" to a spouse, joint tenancy overrides distributions spelled out in Wills.

Joint tenancy exists when two or more people share an interest in personal property or real estate. If the interest is "with right of survivorship," the interest goes to the surviving joint owner, regardless of what a Will says.

Joint tenancy does not take the place of a Will. It applies to a particular piece of property only. A Will can be changed as often as you choose whereas joint tenancy is difficult to change because co-owners must agree to do so once their names are on the property.

Some real problems can develop with a joint tenancy agreement because joint owners (even husband and wife) may disagree. It then becomes difficult to make necessary decisions about management of the property, repairs and division of income. It also affects who inherits your property on death. Even though a Will leaves your property to named individuals, if the bank account or title to real estate is joint with right of survivorship, the joint property will go to the surviving joint owner as previously noted.

Further, joint accounts on deposit in financial institutions are subject to claims to pay debts, taxes and expenses of administration, including statutory allowances to the surviving spouse, minor children and dependent children if other assets of the estate are insufficient. Also, the financial institution may have a lien against the account for any unpaid indebtedness owed it by the deceased.

If the person who dies owns property in addition to that held in joint tenancy, the other property must still be probated. There is also expense involved because a legal proceeding is necessary to transfer title to the surviving owner or owners.

There are no tax savings using joint tenancy. In some larger estates, it can trigger federal estate taxes that could be legally avoided with a properly drafted Will.

LIFE ESTATES

A somewhat popular way of attempting to complete estate planning is the gifting of real property to heirs while retaining a "life estate." Legally, what this means is the donors keep the property and the benefits, including any income from the property, for as long as they live. Then, the property is transferred to the designated owners upon the termination of the life estate (which is the death of the donor).

Thomas Smith and Karen Smith, with Life Estates to Esther and Herman Smith.

Life estates can have significant gift tax or estate tax consequences depending upon the value of the property and the size of the estate. These should not be done without the advice of an estate planning attorney. They can create more legal work than they resolve if improperly done.

A "life estate" has a value and can be sold. Many times elderly relatives entering nursing homes need to sell their life estates to satisfy their financial needs or to qualify for future government support. This does not affect the ultimate owners of the property but does affect the income and benefits of the property while the donor is still alive. Many times the market for life estates is very limited.

It is a helpful estate-planning tool when used in the right circumstances and in the right way.

POD Accounts

Paid on Death or "POD" financial accounts are legal in many states. This is another form used by some to try to uncomplicate estate planning. But the decision to utilize a POD account can face problems with estate and some state gift taxes — again depending upon the size of the estate and number of heirs.

What "POD" means is that upon the death of the owner of the account, the funds will be paid out to the named beneficiary.

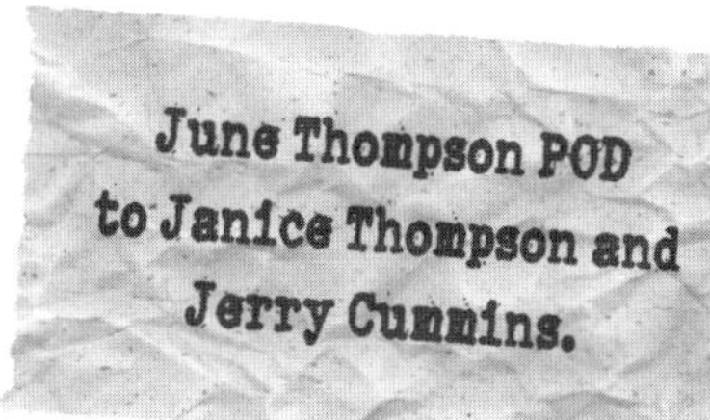

This is another tool that can be useful but cannot be done without professional guidance and all parties fully informed of the effects of the transaction.

Family feuds can break out — along with extra taxes — when a donor names one child on a POD account with verbal instructions to divide the money equally among the heirs. Without any legally binding requirement to do so, an heir who does not follow through can end up with all the money. A lifetime of post-probate feuds can result, and applicable inheritance tax exemptions can be lost.

Who Do You Want Standing In Your Shoes When Decisions Need To Be Made?

POWER OF ATTORNEY!

HOW DOES A LIVING WILL OR DURABLE POWER OF ATTORNEY AFFECT MY ESTATE PLAN?

Insights

"Be on your guard; stand firm in the faith; be men of courage; be strong. Do everything in love."
— I Corinthians 16:13-14

CHAPTER 10

Both Living Wills and Durable Powers of Attorney With Health Powers are considered legally to be "final directives" on how health care decisions should be made during a final illness. These are also commonly called "advanced directives." Both documents establish the guidelines for future health care. While both serve the same purpose, they are vastly different in their functions.

The use of Living Wills or Durable Powers of Attorney With Health Powers have accelerated in recent years. Federal law requires that hospitals, nursing homes, home health agencies, and hospice programs provide patients with written information and policies regarding advanced directives. Many times, decisions on advanced directives are made during a time of medical crisis. Obviously, being able to thoughtfully provide directions to care givers and family as to personal preferences and religious philosophy regarding medical care is important.

WHAT IS A STANDARD POWER OF ATTORNEY?

This document is best described as one that allows another person to "stand in your shoes" doing all things you could do. This generally includes all aspects of handling financial affairs. A Standard Power of Attorney many times is used if someone is going to be temporarily abroad and wants to have another person execute legal documents and conduct financial affairs for him. It is a very serious decision to give someone any "power of attorney" because it authorizes the person to act on your behalf.

The use of the word "attorney" is not in the sense of one licensed to practice law, although it could be. This is a legal term which is given to someone holding the powers given to them in a Power of Attorney document. This can be a spouse, trusted friend or relative.

DURABLE POWER OF ATTORNEY

This is the same as a Standard Power of Attorney, except it remains valid even if you become incompetent or incapacitated. The Durable Power of Attorney terminates upon the death of the maker, but it does carry through when the person is unable to act on his own behalf. It is an important substitute for having an expensive guardianship or conservatorship in the event you become incapacitated. These legal proceedings can be avoided by a properly drafted Durable Power of Attorney.

What is a Durable Power of Attorney With Health Powers?

A Durable Power of Attorney With Health Powers, legally appoints another person who has your Power of Attorney to also act as your health care agent in making any health care decisions that you are incapable of making. This is generally a spouse or trusted member of your family who can work with your doctor in making appropriate decisions.

What is a Living Will?

A Living Will is a document that gives specific instructions to your doctor and other health care providers as to the circumstances under which you want life-sustaining treatment provided, withheld, or withdrawn. It is limited to the time medical providers can terminate life-sustaining treatment.

Since nothing is settled until it is settled right, no matter how unlimited power a man may have, unless he excercises it fairly and justly his actions will return to plague him.

— Frank A. Vanderlip

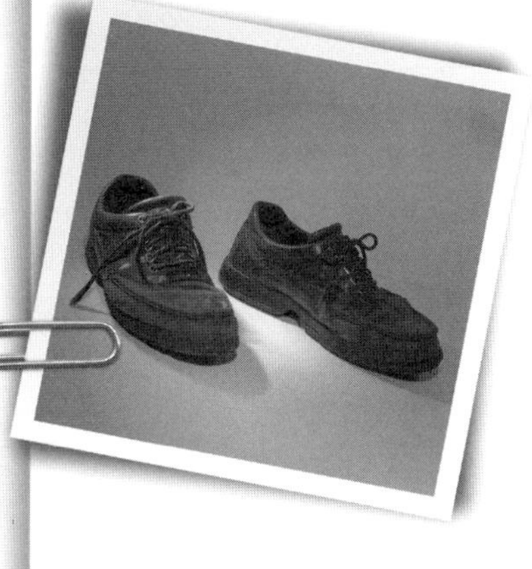

WHICH IS BEST?

Most experts in elder law lean toward a Durable Power of Attorney for health care as a better option than a Living Will. A Durable Power of Attorney for health care can provide everything that can be included in a Living Will but is a more flexible document. Too often, persons wishing life-sustaining treatment to be limited sign a Living Will, which is far too restrictive given the availability of current medical treatment.

A Durable Power of Attorney allows the designated health care agent to work with the attending doctors on the appropriate life-sustaining treatment within the scope of what you have spelled out in making this decision. A Living Will fails in many cases to provide the full range of health care decisions that may need to be made.

In summary, a Durable Power of Attorney for health decisions is a far more comprehensive and flexible document than a Living Will.

DURABLE POWER OF ATTORNEY

The following is an example of a typical Durable Power of Attorney With Health Powers:

WARNING! This is a sample form for discussion purposes only.

KNOW ALL MEN BY THESE PRESENTS: That I, (name), have made, constituted and appointed, and by these presents do make, constitute and appoint (name) my true and lawful attorney in my name, place, and stead, and for my use and benefit, and as my act and deed;

To take possession of, hold, manage, operate, sell, lease, exchange, invest, insure, repair, alter, improve, mortgage, pledge, or otherwise encumber or dispose of, upon such terms and consideration as said attorney may deem proper, any or all of my real or personal property, or any interest therein of whatsoever kind or nature and wheresoever situated, which I now own or hereafter may acquire;

To deposit and withdraw for any purpose in either my said attorney's name or my name or jointly in both our names, in or from any banking institution, any funds, negotiable paper, or monies which may come into my said attorney's hands as such attorney or which I now or hereafter may have on deposit or be entitled to;

To sit as my attorney or proxy in respect to any stocks, shares, bonds or other investments, rights, or interests, I may now or hereafter hold;

To take possession of and order the removal and shipment of any of my property from any post, warehouse, depot, dock, or other place of storage or safekeeping, governmental or private; and to execute and deliver any release, voucher, receipt, shipping ticket, certificate, or other instrument necessary or convenient for such purpose;

To execute and deliver vouchers in my behalf for any and all allowances and reimbursements properly payable to me by the United States, including but not restricted to allowances and reimbursements for transportation of

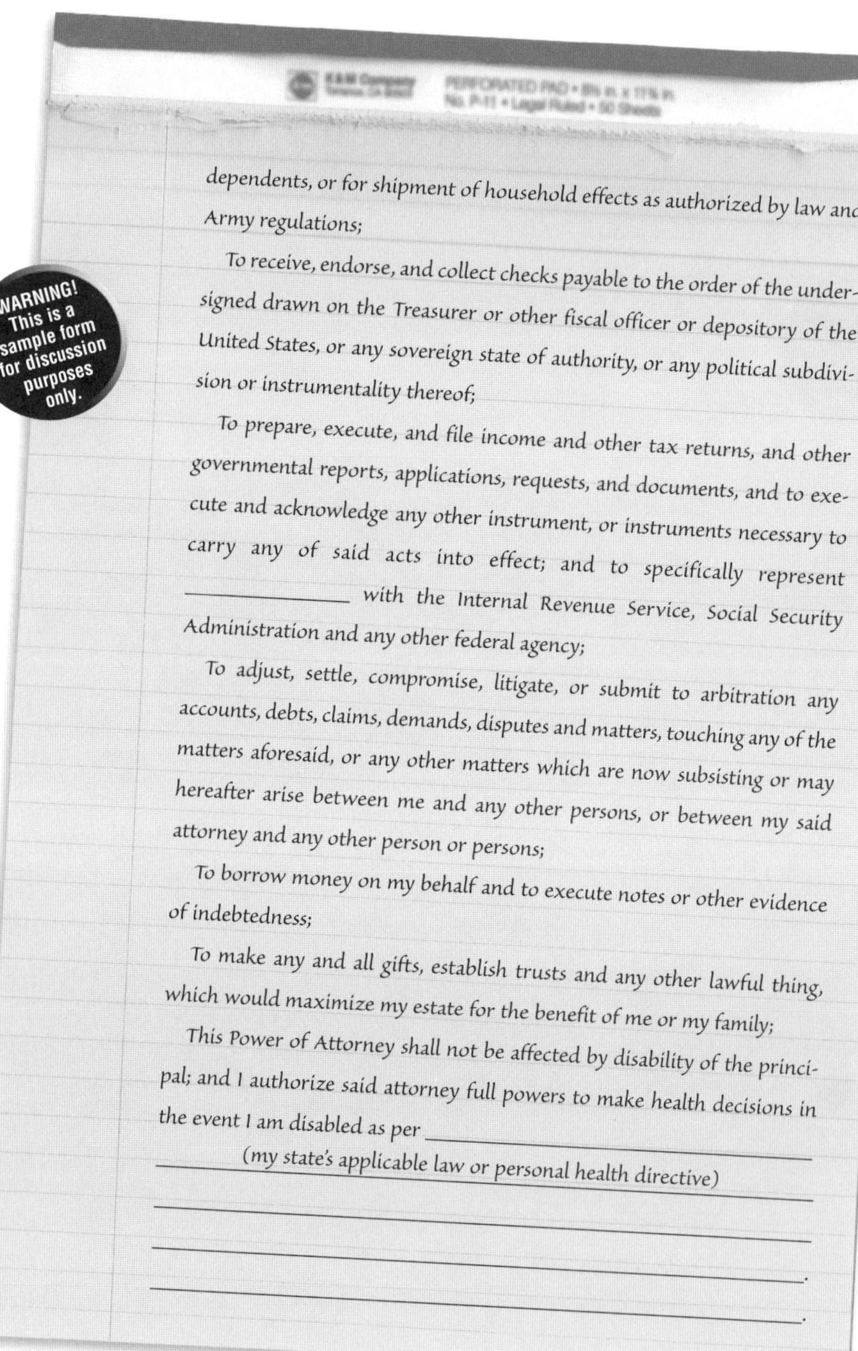

dependents, or for shipment of household effects as authorized by law and Army regulations;

To receive, endorse, and collect checks payable to the order of the undersigned drawn on the Treasurer or other fiscal officer or depository of the United States, or any sovereign state of authority, or any political subdivision or instrumentality thereof;

To prepare, execute, and file income and other tax returns, and other governmental reports, applications, requests, and documents, and to execute and acknowledge any other instrument, or instruments necessary to carry any of said acts into effect; and to specifically represent ______________ with the Internal Revenue Service, Social Security Administration and any other federal agency;

To adjust, settle, compromise, litigate, or submit to arbitration any accounts, debts, claims, demands, disputes and matters, touching any of the matters aforesaid, or any other matters which are now subsisting or may hereafter arise between me and any other persons, or between my said attorney and any other person or persons;

To borrow money on my behalf and to execute notes or other evidence of indebtedness;

To make any and all gifts, establish trusts and any other lawful thing, which would maximize my estate for the benefit of me or my family;

This Power of Attorney shall not be affected by disability of the principal; and I authorize said attorney full powers to make health decisions in the event I am disabled as per ______________________________

(my state's applicable law or personal health directive)

____

____.

____.

WARNING! This is a sample form for discussion purposes only.

GIVING AND GRANTING unto my said attorney full power and authority to do and perform all and every act, deed, matter, and thing whatsoever in and about my said estate, property and affairs as fully and effectually to all intents and purposes as I might or could do in my own proper person if personally present, the above specifically enumerated powers being in aid and exemplifications of the full, complete and general power herein granted and not in limitation of definition thereof; and hereby ratifying all that my said attorney has heretofore done or shall lawfully do or cause to be done by virtue of these present.

IN WITNESS WHEREOF, I have hereunto set my hand and seal this _____ day of ________________, ______.

____

State of ______________)

: ss

County of ____________)

Subscribed and sworn to before me this _____ day of __________, ______.

____

Notary Public

My Commission Expires:

LIVING WILL
The following is an example of a typical Living Will:

TO MY FAMILY, PHYSICIANS, AND ALL THOSE CONCERNED WITH MY CARE:

I, _______________, willfully and voluntarily make this declaration as a directive to be followed if I am in a terminal condition and become unable to participate in decisions regarding my medical care.

With respect to any life-sustaining treatment, I direct the following: (Initial only one of the following optional directives if you agree. If you do not agree with any of the following directives, space is provided below for you to write your own directives.)

___ NO LIFE-SUSTAINING TREATMENT. I direct that no life-sustaining treatment be provided. If life-sustaining treatment is begun, terminate it.

___ TREATMENT FOR RESTORATION. Provide life-sustaining treatment only if and for so long as you believe treatment offers a reasonable possibility of restoring to me the ability to think and act for myself.

___ TREAT UNLESS PERMANENTLY UNCONSCIOUS. If you believe that I am permanently unconscious and are satisfied that this condition is irreversible, then do not provide me with life-sustaining treatment, and if life-sustaining treatment is being provided to me, terminate it. If and so long as you believe that treatment has a reasonable possibility of restoring consciousness to me, then provide life-sustaining treatment.

___ MAXIMUM TREATMENT. Preserve my life as long as possible, but do not provide treatment that is not in accordance with accepted medical standards as then in effect.

(Artificial nutrition and hydration is food and water provided by means of nasogastric tube or tubes inserted into the stomach, intestines, or veins. If

WARNING! This is a sample form for discussion purposes only.

you do not wish to receive this form of treatment, you must initial the statement below which reads: "I intend to include this treatment, among the 'life-sustaining treatment' that may be withheld or withdrawn.")

With respect to artificial nutrition and hydration, I wish to make clear that (initial only one):

____ I intend to include this treatment among the "life-sustaining treatment" that may be withheld or withdrawn.

____ I do not intend to include this treatment among the "life-sustaining treatment" that may be withheld or withdrawn.

(If you do not agree with any of the printed directives and want to write your own, or if you want to write directives in addition to the printed provisions, or if you want to express some of your other thoughts, you can do so here.)

Date: ________________ ________________________
Signature

____
Typed or printed name

____
Address

____

____

WARNING! This is a sample form for discussion purposes only.

Either of these documents can be modified to reflect personal choice. However, the Living Will is far more restrictive.

The declarant voluntarily signed this document in my presence.

Witness: ________________________

Witness: ________________________

Witness: ________________________

Witness: ________________________

Witness: ________________________

On this _____ day of __________, ______, the declarant, __________________, and witnesses __________________ and __________________, personally appeared before the undersigned officer and signed the foregoing instrument in my presence.

Dated this _____ day of ____________, ______.

____
Notary Public
My Commission Expires:

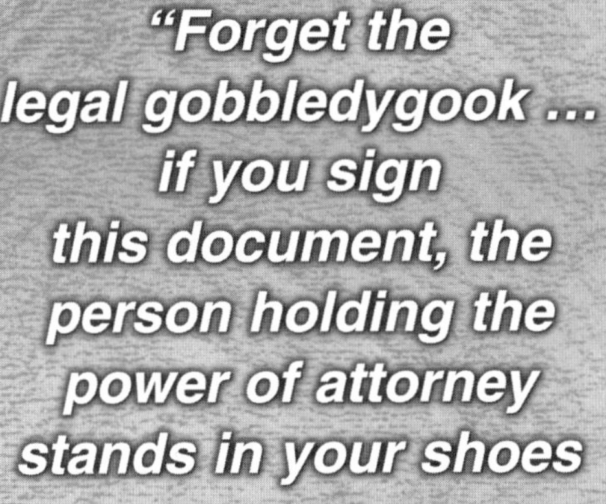

"Forget the
legal gobbledygook ...
if you sign
this document, the
person holding the
power of attorney
stands in your shoes

**and can do
everything
you can do**

including deciding
whether you
live or die
in a health
crisis event."

—Rollyn H. Samp

Some of the frequently asked questions about these documents are as follows:

Can I select a second choice for a health care agent if the first is unable or unwilling to serve?

Yes, that is a common practice in drafting these documents.

Should I tell the person I have selected my feelings on health care decisions?

Absolutely. In drafting this document, you are really asking a person to stand in your shoes and make the same decisions you would make if you were able to make them. This requires a high level of communication between you and the person you have designated as a health care agent.

Can a health care agent make a decision against my wishes or against appropriate medical practice?

No. The person holding your Durable Power of Attorney With Health Powers must follow your wishes and consider the recommendations of the attending physician. Any decision made by your health care agent must be within the scope of accepted medical practice. To avoid confusion, it is suggested a copy be placed in your medical records and a copy be given to the holder of your Durable Power of Attorney.

Is there an approved form for a Durable Power of Attorney?

There are a variety of forms, but not one legally recognized form for this document. It is a document that should be worked out as part of a comprehensive estate plan with your attorney. You should never sign either a Durable Power of Attorney With Health Powers or Living Will form without clearly understanding all the implications of signing this form.

What should be done with my Durable Power of Attorney or Living Will?

Whatever document you sign, it is a good idea to give one copy to your principal physician for your medical record, a copy to the person in your family whom you've designated to be in charge of your affairs, and many people wish to give a copy to their pastor or priest. Normally, your attorney will also keep a copy which can be telefaxed nearly anywhere in the world!

Can I revoke a Durable Power of Attorney or a Living Will?

Yes, but this must be done in writing. If you revoke one of these documents, it is important that those who have copies of the previous document get copies of the new document or a letter stating that the original document has been revoked.

Can I amend a Durable Power of Attorney for Health Care or Living Will?

Yes. This can be done at any time as long as you have the mental capacity to make these decisions.

The decisions made regarding a Living Will, Durable Power of Attorney With Health Powers and organ donation represent, literally, life and death decisions. Consultation with an attorney experienced in elder law and your personal physician are important parts of the estate-planning process. These decisions are best made before the trauma of a life-threatening health event. These still require the same decisions but often lack the processes and too frequently fail to reflect the personal wishes of the individual.

"... seeing again, is really believing again in the goodness of God's people."

As *Christ* gave His life for us, our useable organs at our death can be a gift of life for others.

"... a whole life to live because someone cared enough to give."

"... a second chance at life with a replacement heart unleashes a talent nearly lost to disease."

HOW ORGAN DONATIONS CAN BE A LIVING GIFT

Living Gifts

"Be joyful always; pray continually; give thanks in all circumstances, for this is God's will for you in Christ Jesus."
— I Thessalonians 5:16-18

CHAPTER 11

The joy of making a decision to become an organ donor is a step in completing a viable estate plan. This is an appropriate time to discuss organ donation, which has become a growing trend in giving beyond life.

Considering the tremendous opportunities for others to continue life or live a better life, a wonderful act of love and stewardship is sharing upon death those organs suitable for use. Organ donation can be set out in the Durable Power of Attorney, Living Will or done on separate forms for organ donation.

As medical technology advances, the ability to save and extend lives through organ donations is accelerating.

Most Christian churches support the personal decisions of organ donation as an act of love, charity, and ministry to others. As Christ gave His life for us, our useable organs at our death can be a gift of life to others. There is no specific doctrinal mandate to be an organ donor, but just as the gift of physical property is a personal decision so is the decision of organ donation.

Modern medicine can use far more organs than it can obtain. A new name is added to the national waiting list for organ donation every 16 minutes. On average, ten people a day die awaiting organ transplants. One organ donor has the potential for saving the lives of up to eight people.

A national registry for organ donation has been developed through the United Network for Organ Sharing (UNOS Website: www.unos.org).

In 1999, for example, there were 66,000 persons on the national waiting list illustrating the need for these gifts:

Kidney	43,403
Liver	13,060
Pancreas	447
Kidney-Pancreas	1,900
Heart	4,254
Heart-Lung	249
Lung	3,279
Intestines	120

The greatest barrier to the gift of organ donation is the lack of understanding of the needs and lack of communication to doctors and family of a person's desire to make this part of a "final tithe." Several regional organizations promote and assist in organ donation. LifeSource Upper Midwest Organ Procurement Organization, Inc.[7] have produced helpful questions and answers for potential donors.

[7] LifeSource, 2550 University Avenue West, Suite 315, South Saint Paul, Minnesota 55114-1904.

What Are the Common Misconceptions About Organ Donation?

When I die, the doctors and nurses will not be aware that I want to be a donor.

In the case of organ donation, permission from your family is essential. Therefore, tell your family your decision so they can see that your wishes are fulfilled. Designating your wishes on your driver's license or signing a donor card are good first steps, but take that next step and have the important conversation about donation with your family today.

If I'm carrying a donor card or if "DONOR" is on my driver's license and I'm admitted to a hospital, they may let me die so they can recover my organs.

There is no conflict between saving lives and recovering organs for lifesaving transplants. The doctors and nurses who try to save your life are not the same specialists involved in transplantation. Organ donation is offered as an option to your family only after all lifesaving measures have failed and you have been declared legally dead. In order to donate organs, a patient must be declared brain dead. Brain death is death. It is the complete and irreversible loss of all brain function. Using specific medical criteria, a physician can confirm brain death beyond any doubt.

If I'm in a coma or vegetative state, they may recover my organs.

Patients in a coma or vegetative state do not meet medical criteria as potential donors since they still have some brain function and, therefore, are still alive. Potential organ donors must be declared brain dead.

There is a "black market" for organs in the United States.

According to the Anatomical Gift Act of 1968, it is illegal to buy or sell human organs. In addition, every organ donation and transplant is reviewed by a national governing body. Strict regulations prevent any type of "black market" from existing in the United States. Organs must be recovered only by a federally designated organ procurement organization.

My family will have to pay for the cost of my organ donation.

There is no cost to the donor family for donation. All expenses related to organ donation are assumed by governmentally designated organ-procurement organizations and passed on to the organ transplant recipients and their health insurers. However, funeral

The Joy of Sharing Your Life:

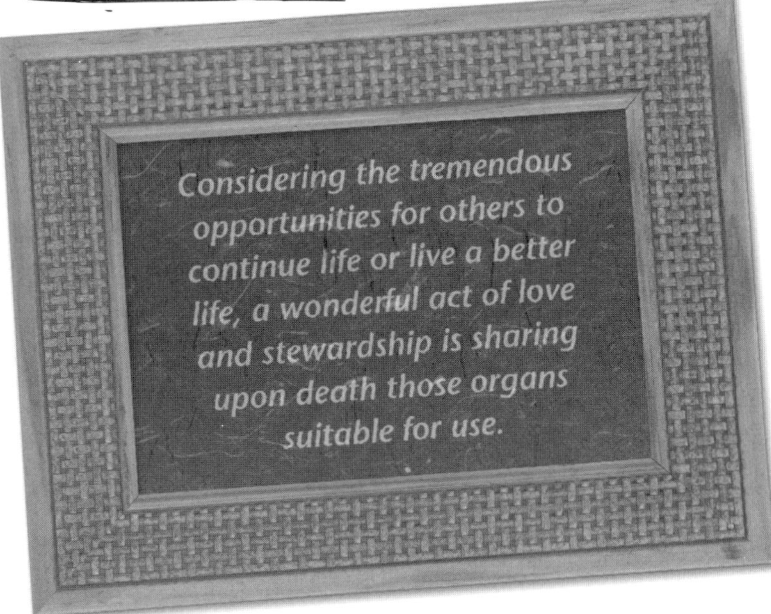

expenses and hospital costs not associated with the donation remain the family's responsibility.

My body will look different if I donate my organs.

Donation is a surgical procedure. The body's natural appearance is maintained. As in any other medical procedure, the body is treated with great respect and dignity.

If I am a donor, I won't be able to have a regular, open-casket funeral service.

Donation does not delay funeral arrangements. You may have an open-casket service.

The rich and famous have a better chance of receiving a transplant.

Eligibility to receive an organ transplant is not determined by a person's financial or celebrity status. After a patient has been determined to be a medically suitable candidate for an organ transplant, his or her name is added to the national computer waiting list. Organs are fairly allocated based upon medical urgency, blood type, weight, size, genetic typing, and length of time on the waiting list.

Other Important Questions About Organ Donation

Who manages organ donations?

Non-patient, federally designated organ-procurement organizations. Often referred to as the "matchmaker," these organizations make the medical "matches" between patients who have died and whose families have donated their organs with patients waiting for organ transplants. Funding for organ donation services is derived from standard procurement fees paid by the transplant centers. There is no cost to donor families for donation.

What organs are needed for donation?

Organs that can be donated are the heart, lungs, liver, kidneys, pancreas, eyes, and small intestines. One organ donor can save the lives of eight people.

How successful are transplants?

There are more than 19,000 organ transplants performed in the United States annually. Transplants have become a successful form of treatment for end-stage organ disease. Three-year patient success rates are estimated at 95 percent for kidney transplants, 92 percent for pancreas transplants, 91 percent for heart transplants, 90 percent for liver transplants, 81 percent for heart-lung transplants, and 76 percent for lung transplants.

Why is it important for more African Americans and Native Americans to become organ donors?

Successful kidney transplantation is often enhanced by matching organs between members of the same ethnic or racial group. Approximately one-third of the individuals waiting for kidney transplants are African-American. Why? African Americans are 17 times more likely than Caucasians to develop hypertension which can lead to eventual kidney failure. Also, a higher incidence of hypertension and diabetes among Native Americans increases the risk of kidney failure for this segment of the population.

What are the benefits of organ donation?

Families who make the decision to donate often find that donation helps them through their grieving process. They receive great personal benefit by being able to have something positive come from the death of a loved one. For recipients, organ transplants offer a second chance at life, enabling them and their families to maintain a more normal, higher quality of life.

"The thief comes only to steal and kill and destroy; I have come that they may have life, and have it to the full. I am the good shepherd. The good shepherd lays down his life for the sheep."

John 10:10-11

How do I become an organ donor?

Tell your family your wishes. It's that simple. In the event of your death, your next-of-kin's permission must be obtained. An organ donor card or your driver's license are only indications of your wishes. Family consent must still be obtained.

What can I do if a member of my family becomes a potential organ donor?

If no one on the medical team suggests organ donation, you, as the next of kin, should inform the medical staff of your wishes. Organs will only be removed if there is written permission from the family.

Who is considered my next of kin?

The following prioritized list determines who would give permission for donation: spouse, adult son or daughter, either parent, adult brother or sister, grandparent, legal guardian, medical examiner.

What is the criteria for becoming an organ donor?

Organs can be donated only after a person has been declared brain dead while their vital organs are being maintained on a breathing machine.

Should my age or health condition influence my decision to become an organ donor?

While medical history and age are factors, most people can donate. People with diabetes, hepatitis, and cancer sometimes can donate their organs. The only individuals who cannot donate are those who test positive for HIV. Age criteria for organ donation is evaluated on an individual basis.

Is there a main registry for organ donors?

There is no official organ donor registry. Although there are a few "registries" in existence in the United States, these are utilized as tools to promote donation awareness. They are not accessed during the organ donation process since permission must be received from the next of kin.

How are organs distributed to patients waiting for organ transplants?

Every person waiting for an organ transplant is registered with UNOS, the United Network for Organ Sharing. UNOS manages the computerized network to match organ donors with waiting recipients.

When a family gives permission for organ donation, the responsible organ-procurement organization inputs medical information about the organ donor into a database and prints a computerized match list of potential recipients. Matching is based upon medical criteria such as blood type, weight, size of the organ, length of time waiting for a transplant, and severity of the illness. Genetic (tissue) matching is also a key factor for kidney and pancreas transplants. A person's sex, race, ethnicity, social or financial status play absolutely no role in the organ matching process.

Life

Jesus said, "I have come that they may have life, and have it to the full."

— John 10:10

Do any organs go to waste?

Donated organs are "matched" with transplant recipients before they are removed for transplant. Extensive tests before surgery determine which organs can be recovered; however physicians can't always tell if the organ is suitable until surgery takes place. If the organ is unsuitable for transplantation at the time of donation, the organ is not recovered from the donor.

Can organs be used for research?

If an organ cannot be used for transplantation, it may be useful for research. Research often helps the medical community in its effort to find cures for diseases such as cancer, or find help for a health condition such as diabetes. Written permission from the next of kin must be obtained for research.

How do family members respond when the possibility of organ donation is discussed at the time of a loved one's death?

Grief-stricken family members have often said their sorrow has been eased by the knowledge that their personal tragedy gave new life to another person and that it provided some meaning to an otherwise senseless death. Many more families today are raising the issue of organ donation themselves because they are aware of its lifesaving value.

What is brain death?

Brain death is death. It occurs when the brain and the brain stem stop functioning. Examples of injuries that cause brain death include trauma to the head from a bike or motor vehicle accident, a ruptured blood vessel in the brain, or drowning. A person can only become an organ donor if he or she dies from a brain death injury.

> "Living Wills" should be very specific about the definition of "brain dead" and not so carelessly worded that they can be enacted by greedy heirs if your foot goes to sleep.
>
> — P.J. O'Rourke

The brain is an organ like all the other organs in the body. It requires a steady blood supply to deliver the oxygen and nutrients it needs to do its work. When the brain cells do not receive enough oxygen or nutrients, they die. Once the brain cells die, there is no chance for recovery.

Cardiac death is different than brain death. Cardiac death happens when the heart and lungs stop functioning. People who die from cardiac death cannot donate their organs because of deterioration due to lack of oxygen. Eye and tissue donations are, however, options.

Is brain death the same as a coma or vegetative state?

A person in a coma or vegetative state still has some brain activity and, therefore, has not died.

Why must artificial support continue after brain death has been determined?

The respirator or breathing machine provides oxygen to the organs keeping them healthy until they are removed for transplant.

How long can organs be preserved for transplantation after their removal?

Once the organs have been removed, they are cooled and preserved. Organs can be preserved for varying amounts of time: heart and lungs, 4-6 hours; liver, pancreas and intestines, 12-24 hours; kidney, up to 36 hours.

Will the identity of the organ donor be revealed to the transplant recipient?

Generally, no. The identities of both the recipient and the donor family are confidential. The donation coordinator sends a letter to the donor family informing them about the organ recipients, such as their age and sex, and how their health has improved. Some donor families and recipients correspond anonymously. On occasions, when both sides wish to meet, the donation coordinator will help facilitate such meetings.

How Do You Become an Organ Donor?

Advising your family and family doctor of your decision is the most important step after making the decision. Donor organizations have prepared donor cards and family witness cards to assist in this process. The following are samples:

I want to Share My Life!
Organ/Tissue Donor Card

I, ____________________, would like to be an organ donor at the time of my death. I have told my family my decision and understand that their permission is necessary for organ donation to take place. I have asked my family to honor my wishes. *These family members are witnesses of my commitment to organ donation:*

Donor Signature: ____________________ Date__________

Witness: ____________________

Witness: ____________________

Keep this card as a reminder of your decision to help save lives.

I want to Share My Life!
Family Witness Card

This card is to inform you that I would like to be an organ donor at the time of my death. Since my family's permission is necessary for organ donation to take place, please see that my decision is carried out. Thank you for respecting my wishes.

Donor Signature: ____________________ Date__________

Give this card to a family member as a reminder of your decision to save lives through organ donation.

In many states, donors are listed on driver's licenses. But these are only indications of wishes and still require permission by the next of kin. Again, because time is important, just having your wishes known within your Will may be inadequate since Wills may not be reviewed until several days after death.

i am making everything new:

Revelation 21:5

How to Obtain Additional Information on Organ Donation

The following are contact points for additional information on organ donation, or you may contact any major hospital that has a person knowledgeable in organ donation who can assist in answering your questions and providing information for you:

Alabama Organ Center 301 South 20th Street, Suite 1001, Birmingham, AL 35233-2033; phone 205-731-9200/9250; fax 205-731-9250.

Arkansas Regional Organ Recovery Agency 1100 North University, Suite 200, Little Rock, AR 72207-6344; phone 501-224-2623; fax 501-372-6279.

Donor Network of Arizona 3877 North Seventh Street, Suite 200, Phoenix, AZ 85014; phone 602-222-2200; fax 602-222-2202.

California Transplant Donor Network 55 Francisco Street, Suite 510, San Francisco, CA 94133- 2115; phone 415-837-5888; fax 415-837-5880.

Golden State Donor Services 1760 Creekside Oaks Drive, Suite 160, Sacramento, CA 95833- 3632; phone 916-567-1600; fax 916-567-8300.

Southern California Organ Procurement Center 2200 West Third Street, Suite 200, Los Angeles, CA 90057; main phone 213-413-6219; fax 213-413-5373.

Regional Organ Procurement Agency of Southern California 11150 West Olympic Boulevard, Suite 770, Los Angeles, CA 90064-1824; phone 310-206-0222; fax 310-825-5512.

Organ and Tissue Acquisition Center of Southern California 3665 Ruffin Road, Suite 120, San Diego, CA 92123; phone 619-292-8750; fax 619-560-5945.

Donor Alliance 3773 Cherry Creek North Drive, Suite 601, Denver, CO 80209; phone 303-329- 4747; fax 303-321-1183.

Northeast Organ Procurement Organization and Tissue Bank Hartford Hospital, 80 Seymour Street, P. O. Box 5037, Hartford, CT 06102-5037; phone 860-545-2256; fax 860-545-4143.

Washington Regional Transplant Consortium 8110 Gatehouse Road, Suite 101 West, Falls Church, VA 22042; phone 703-641-0100; fax 703-641-0211.

Translife 2501 North Orange Avenue, #40, Orlando, FL 32817; phone 407-897-5560; fax 407- 897-5574.

University of Miami Organ Procurement Organization 1150 NW 14th Street, Suite 208, Miami, FL 33136; phone 305-243-7622; fax 305-243-7628.

Lifelink of Southwest Florida 12573 New Brittany Boulevard, Fort Myers, FL 33907-3625; phone 941-936-2772; fax 941-936-6330.

Organ Procurement Organization at University of Florida 1600 Archer Road SE, P. O. Box 100163, Gainsville, FL 32610-0163; phone 352-395-0632; fax 352-338-9886.

Lifelink of South Florida 3021 West Swann Avenue, Tampa, FL 33609; phone 813-348-6308; fax 813-348-0571.

Lifelink of Georgia 3715 Northside Parkway, Suite 300, Atlanta, GA 30327; phone 404-266- 8884; fax 404-266-0592.

Organ Donor Center of Hawaii 1000 Bishop Street, Suite 302, Honolulu, HI 96813; phone 808- 599-7630; fax 808-533-7631.

Iowa Statewide Organ Procurement Organization 2732 Northgate Drive, Iowa City, IA 52245; phone 319-377-7515; fax 319-337-6105.

Regional Organ Bank of Illinois 800 South Wells, Suite 190, Chicago, IL 60607-4529; phone 312-431-3600; fax 312-803-7643.

Indiana Organ Procurement Organization 429 North Pennsylvania Street, Suite 201, Indianapolis, IN 46204-1816; phone 317-685-0389; fax 317-685-1687.

Kentucky Organ Donor Affiliates 106 East Broadway, Louisville, KY 40202; phone 502-581- 9511; fax 502-589-5157.

Louisiana Organ Procurement Agency 3501 North Causeway Boulevard, Suite 940, Metairie, LA 70002-3626; phone 504-837-3355; fax 504-837-3587.

New England Organ Bank Washington Street at Newton Corner, One Gateway Center, Newton, MA 02158-2803; phone 617-244-8000; fax 617-244-8755.

Transplant Resources Center of Maryland 1540 Caton Center Drive, Suite R, Baltimore, MD 21227; phone 410-242-7000; fax 410-242-1871.

Transplantation Society of Michigan 2203 Platt Road, Ann Arbor, MI 48104; phone 734-973- 1577; fax 734-973-3133

Lifesource Upper Midwest Organ Procurement Organization 2550 University Avenue West, Suite 315 South, St. Paul, MN 55114-1904; phone 612-603-7800; fax 612-603-7801.

Mid American Transplant Services 1139 Olivette Executive Parkway, St. Louis, MO 63132- 3205; phone 314-991-1661; fax 314-991-2805.

Mississippi Organ Recovery Agency 12 River Bend Place, Suite B, Jackson, MS 39208; phone 601-933-1000; fax 601-933-1006.

Midwest Organ Bank 1900 West 47th Place, Suite 400, Westwood, KS 66205; phone 913-262- 1666; fax 913-262-5130.

Carolina Lifecare Westbrook Plaza Drive, Suite 200, Winston Salem, NC 27103; phone 336- 774-4450; fax 336-774-6591.

Lifeshare of the Carolinas Carolinas Medical Center, 101 WT Harris Boulevard, Suite 5302, P. O. Box 32861, Charlotte, NC 28262; phone 704-548-6850; fax 704-548-6851.

Carolina Organ Procurement Agency 702 Johns Hopkins Drive, Greenville, NC 27834; phone 919-757-0090; fax 919-757-0708.

Nebraska Organ Retrieval System Inc. 4060 Vinton Street, Suite 200, Omaha, NE 68105; phone 402-553-7952; fax 402-553-0933.

New Jersey Organ and Tissue Sharing Network Organ Procurement Organization 841 Mountain Avenue, Springfield, NJ 07081; phone 973-379-4535; fax 973-379-5113.

New Mexico Donor Program 2715 Broadbent Parkway NE, Suite J, Albuquerque, NM 87107- 1609; phone 505-843-7672; fax 505-343-1828.

Nevada Donor Network 4580 South Eastern Avenue, Suite 33, Las Vegas, NV 89119; phone 702-796-9600; fax 702-796-4225.

Center for Donation and Transplant 218 Great Oaks Boulevard, Albany, NY 12203; phone 518- 262-5606; fax 518-262-5427.

Finger Lakes Donor Recovery Program Corporate Woods of Brighton, Building 120, Suite 180, Rochester, NY 14623; phone 716-272-4930; fax 716-272-4956.

New York Organ Donor Network 475 Riverside Drive, Suite 1244, New York, NY 10115-1244; phone 212-870-2240; fax 212-870-3299.

Upstate New York Transplant Services Inc. 165 Genesee Street, Suite 102, Buffalo, NY 14203; phone 716-853-6667; fax 716-853-6674.

LifeBanc 20600 Chagrin Boulevard, Suite 350, Cleveland, OH 44122-5343; phone 216-752- 5433; fax 216-751-4204.

Life Connection of Ohio 1545 Holland Road, Suite C, Maumee, OH 43537-1694; phone 419- 893-4891; fax 419-893-1827.

Lifeline of Ohio 770 Kinnear Road, Suite 200, Columbus, OH 43212; phone 614-291-5667; fax 614-291-0660.

Ohio Valley Lifecenter 2925 Vernon Place, Suite 300; Cincinnati, OH 45219-2430; phone 513- 558-5555; fax 513-558-5556.

Oklahoma Organ Sharing Network 5801 North Broadway, Suite 100, Oklahoma City, OK 73118-7489; phone 800-241-4483; fax 405-840-9748.

Pacific Northwest Transplant Bank 2611 SW Third Avenue, Suite 320, Portland, OR 97201- 4952; phone 503-494-5560; fax 503-494-4725.

Gift of Life Donor Program 2000 Hamilton Street, Suite 201, Rodin Place, Philadelphia, PA 19130-3813; phone 215-557-8090; fax 215-557-9359.

Center for Organ Recovery and Education 204 Sigma Drive, RIDC Park, Pittsburgh, PA 15238- 2825; phone 412-963-3550; fax 412-963-3563.

Lifelink of Puerto Rico Digital Plaza, Suite 402, Metro Office Park, Guaynabo, PR 00968-1702; phone 787-277-0900; fax 787-277-0876.

South Carolina Organ Procurement Agency 1064 Gardner Road, Suite 105, Charleston, SC 29407; phone 803-763-7755; fax 803-763-6393.

Tennessee Donor Services 1714 Hayes Street, Nashville, TN 37203; phone 615-327-2247; fax 615-320-1655.

Mid South Transplant Foundation 910 Madison Avenue, Suite 805, Memphis, TN 38103; phone 910-488-4588; fax 901-448-8126.

LifeGift Organ Donation Center 5615 Kirby Drive, Suite 900, Houston, TX 77005-2405; phone 713-523-4438; fax 713-737-8100.

Texas Organ Sharing Alliance 8122 Datapoint Drive, Suite 1150, San Antonio, TX 78229; phone 210-614-7030; fax 210-614-2129.

Southwest Transplant Alliance 3710 Rawlins, #1100, Dallas, TX 75219; phone 214-522-0255; fax 214-552-0430.

Intermountain Organ Recovery System 230 South 500 East, Suite 290, Salt Lake City, UT 84102; phone 801-521-1755; fax 801-364-8815.

Virginias Organ Procurement Agency 1527 Huguenot Road, Suite 102, Midlothian, VA 23113; phone 804-134-7122; fax 804-379-0304.

Lifenet 5809 Ward Court, Virginia Beach, VA 23455; phone 757-464-4761; fax 757-464-5721.

Lifecenter Northwest 2553 SE 76th Avenue, Mercer Island, WA 98040; phone 206-230-5767; fax 206-230-5806.

Wisconsin Donor Network 9200 West Wisconsin Avenue, Milwaukee, WI 53226; phone 414- 259-2024; fax 414-259-8059.

Organ Procurement Organization at University of Wisconsin 600 Highland Avenue, F4/316, Madison, WI 53792; phone 608-263-1341; fax 608-262-9099.

Balance Sheets per Books
Assets
End of tax year
Saturday
April
15
IRS
Department of the Treasury
THE IRS MISSION
PROVIDE AMERICA'S
TAXPAYERS TOP QUALITY
SUMMARY OF YEARLY LIVING EXPENSES
NET WORTH
8
Evaluate
MONTHLY EXPENSE CHART
SAVINGS SUMMARY
INCOME
BUDGET
FINANCIAL
CONFIDENTIAL
Examinations, Appeals, Collections, and Refunds
"No-Tax Trust"

HOW FEDERAL TAXES CAN AFFECT ESTATE PLANS

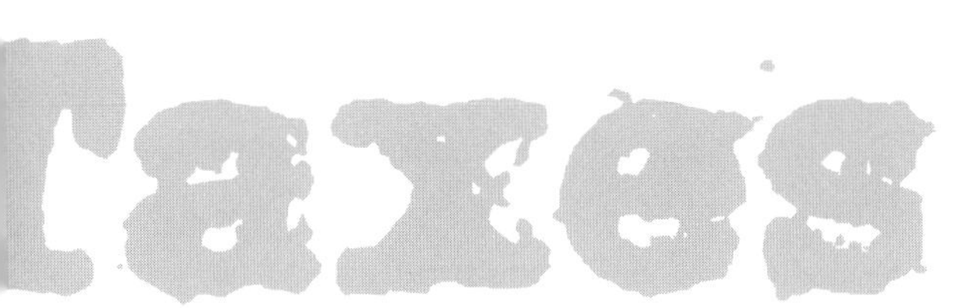

"Then he said to them, 'Give to Caesar what is Caesar's, and to God what is God's.'"
— Matthew 22:21.

CHAPTER 12

Jesus was clear in his direction to pay government what it legally had coming, He did not say it was necessary to overpay.

The federal government levies a tax on estates based on the value of the estates at the time of death with various exemptions and rates. Many states tax inheritance, which is a second tax on many estates. A third possible tax on inheritance comes under the complex rules of "step-up basis" for larger estates, which can create capital gains upon the sale of assets by the heir.

The federal estate and gift taxes have gone through a major revision in 2001. Many of the provisions in the tax changes do not take effect immediately but are phased in over ten years.

While the public perception is that the federal estate taxes have been repealed, that is not correct. For ten years, depending upon the value of an estate and if Congress makes no more changes, the federal estate tax will be zero on some estates by 2006 with total repeal in 2010. But then the current federal estate tax law "sunsets;" meaning by or during 2011 Congress will have to re-enact the tax repeal or else the provisions of the pre-2001-act federal estate tax law will automatically become law. This leaves much of estate planning for the next several years in limbo on larger estates.

Even on what appears to be smaller estates, a $700,000 net estate value today can turn into over $1.3 million or more if invested properly for ten years. So most estate planners are urging a flexible estate plan to meet whatever changes the federal government ultimately enacts using the current law as a starting basis.

Because of these changes, anyone with an estate of over $1 million or having the potential to receive inheritance or grow an estate to $1 million or more needs to have professional guidance from an estate planner familiar with the intricacies of federal estate tax law. For illustration purposes, the chart on the following page demonstrates how various-sized estates are currently affected by the new federal tax law until 2001.

One veteran estate planner observed that for wealthy people there is only one good year to die — 2010!

For married couples, there remains no federal estate tax on any size of estate on the first spouse to die. The federal estate tax can become a problem when the second spouse dies. For couples having over $1 million net worth in 2002, using the "No Tax Trust™" concept can preserve the first spouse's applicable exclusion and, in effect, double the exemption for the couple's estate. Without using a will or trust that provides for use of this exclusion, the first-to-die's applicable federal tax exclusion can be lost.

Federal Tax On Net Value of Estate

Year	$2 Million	$3 Million	$4 Million	$5 Million
2001	$560,250	$930,000	$2,170,250	$4,920,250
2002	$435,000	$925,000	$1,930,000	$4,430,000
2003	$435,000	$705,000	$1,905,000	$4,355,000
2004	$225,000	$695,000	$1,665,000	$4,065,000
2005	$225,000	$460,000	$1,635,000	$3,985,000
2006	$0	$450,000	$1,380,000	$3,680,000
2007	$0	$450,000	$1,350,000	$3,600,000
2008	$0	$0	$1,350,000	$3,600,000
2009	$0	$0	$675,000	$2,925,000
2010	$0	$0	$0	$0
2011	$435,000	$945,000	$2,045,000	$4,795,000

Here's an example of the difference for a couple having a $2 million total estate in 2002 under the new law:

Example 1: A husband has $1 million net worth in his name and his wife has the same. The husband dies with a simple Will giving everything to his spouse. There is no tax upon his death. But if the husband dies first, the wife's estate increases from a net worth of $1 million to $2 million. Assuming the same value on the estate with no growth or utilization of other estate-planning tools, the couple's hard-earned, lifetime work will be taxed as follows:

Illustration:	**$2,000,000**	**Wife's estate**
	-1,000,000	**Wife's exemption**
	$1,000,000	**Taxable estate**

Explanation: If the wife died in 2002–2003, her $2 million taxable estate would incur approximately $435,000 in federal estate taxes. The heirs would receive $1,565,000 of their $2 million estate.

Example 2: If the same couple with the same net worth were to utilize the No Tax Trust™, which is a legal means of avoiding federal estate tax, the tax could be avoided. In this example, again the husband is presumed to have died first and there would be no tax to the spouse. However, using the No Tax Trust™, which preserves the applicable exclusion from tax, the following would be the result:

Illustration:

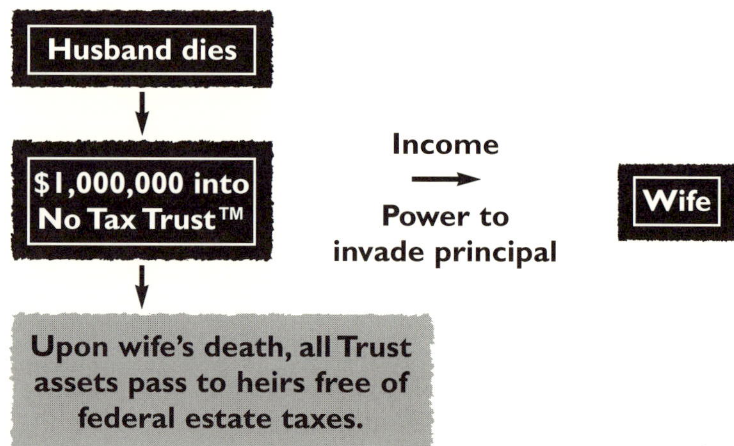

Explanation: Upon the husband's death, $1 million is placed into a No Tax Trust™. The wife receives income for life from the trust and she can invade the principal of the trust under certain circumstances. When the wife dies, the trust (including all accumulation) is not included in the wife's estate and passes to the heirs free of federal estate tax. The wife's estate is $1 million (instead of $2 million as in Example 1) and passes to heirs free of federal estate tax because it does not exceed federal exemption for estate tax in 2002 of $1 million per person.

In this example, the family has saved approximately $330,800 in federal estate taxes and pays nothing!

This example shows that with some very basic estate planning, a family can legally avoid having the federal government take unnecessary taxes. This foresight in estate planning alone can provide a substantial sum of money if a family chooses to do a proper estate plan, increasing the amount of money available for heirs and a final tithe.

The following are the current federal estate tax and gift tax rates which can severely diminish larger estates or those taxable estates failing to use the No Tax Trust™ concept in Will preparation.

New Tax Rates for Taxable Gifts and Transfers at Death

Year	Estate tax and GST death time transfer exemption	Maximum estate and gift tax rate
2002	$1,000,000	50%
2003	$1,000,000	49%
2004	$1,500,000	48%
2005	$1,500,000	47%
2006	$2,000,000	46%
2007-2008	$2,000,000	45%
2009	$3,500,000	45%
2010	N/A (taxes repealed)	Highest individual income tax rate (for gift tax only)
2011 (if reinstated)	$1,000,000	55%

Congress did not stop with just revising federal estate taxes. Little known to many are the federal gift tax laws.

Many couples think they will avoid estate taxes by making lifetime gifts to children or grandchildren. And this can be done. In fact, it is a popular tool to minimize federal estate taxes for larger estates.

First, any taxpayer can give an annual gift of up to $11,000 per person ($22,000 per couple). There is no tax on this transfer, although keeping a record of these gifts is recommended. Split gifts do require a gift tax return.

Secondly, gifts above the annual exclusion can be deducted from the lifetime exemption. That exemption was frozen in the new law at $1 million per person. Starting in 2010, the $1 million lifetime exemption will be indexed for inflation and taxable gifts will be subject to a 35 percent gift tax.

> **...all contributions to qualified churches and religious organizations are deductible from federal estate tax before calculating the net taxable value of an estate.**

While estate and gift taxes currently affect only those with larger estates, Congress could change the provisions any year. And an estate plan which appears to fit perfectly for a family in 2002 could become obsolete if there is a change in the direction of federal law which has been moving to exempt federal estate taxes.

Because of the complexity, this is an area of estate planning that should be handled by those who specialize in federal estate tax law, such as attorneys, CPAs, life insurance agents who have specialized training in this area, or certified financial planners or other professionals who have received certified training and work with this area of the law on a daily basis.

It should be noted that in any scenario, all contributions to qualified churches and religious organizations are deductible from federal estate tax before calculating the net taxable value of an estate.

These are just the basic rudiments of legally avoiding federal estate taxes. There are a variety of hybrid estate plans that can meet individual needs. The purpose of these illustrations is not to provide specific legal advice, but to show there are ways to use the law to increase available funds for a family and the Lord's work by doing a proper estate plan.

As noted in the 2001 tax law and subsequent amendments, federal laws are frequently changing so periodic reviews of your estate plans to check how these changes might affect you and your family are important.

An Education Legacy

For parents and grandparents who believe part of their legacy should be well-educated heirs, the new federal tax law substantially improved ways to help fund higher education choices. These improvements include:

Qualified Education Deduction. For parents whose adjusted gross income does not exceed $130,000 in 2003 and 2004, a deduction for higher education costs up to $3,000 will be allowed. In 2004 and 2005, this will increase to $4,000; and for joint tax filers whose adjusted gross income does not exceed $160,000, they will be allowed an annual qualified education deduction of $2,000.

Education IRAs. The maximum contribution to education IRAs is increased to $2,000 annually with several other positive changes on using this education expense vehicle.

Prepaid Tuition Plans. For "qualified tuition programs," Congress liberalized the laws allowing more parents to help fund education expenses using this vehicle.

Deduction of Student Loan Interest. The ability to deduct the interest on student loans has been increased.

Funding Section 529 Plans. One of the best methods to fund post-secondary education expenses is the funding of what is called a "Section 529" plan. Under this plan, any parent, grandparent, or defined relative can fund the plan. It is one legal method to both make a potential gift and receive tax breaks on earnings. Up to $50,000 per year may be placed in a qualified Section 529 investment. These funds can be used to prepay tuition or be placed in an investment account. When the student decides to enroll in post-secondary education, the funds pay for college tax free. The donor reduces taxable income each year the money is placed in the account. If the funds are not used, they come back to the donor and earnings are taxed as income in the year they are returned but without any penalty. Beneficiaries can be changed on the account and there is no tax to the recipient.

There are numerous other steps which can be taken to make investment in education a part of a family legacy. Since many Christian colleges and seminaries have growing tuition costs, these tax choices make it possible to soften the blow of the costs associated with post-secondary education.

Most financial aid officers, trust officers, financial planners, brokers, insurance agents, CPA's, and other estate planners are very familiar with both the options and complex IRS rules for taking advantage of these choices. Ultimately, they offer a way to make receiving an education an important family legacy for those families who want to encourage this by providing tremendous financial incentives.

If God gave you ten times what you gave Him could you live on it?

Do we?

Make no little plans.
There is nothing in
little plans that
stirs men's blood.
Make big plans.
Once a big idea
is recorded
it can never die.

– Daniel Burham

WHY DYNASTY TRUSTS™ ARE BECOMING A POPULAR ESTATE-PLANNING TOOL

"He who fears the Lord has a secure fortress, and for his children it will be a refuge."
— Proverbs 14:26

CHAPTER 13

If you were told it is possible to shelter millions of dollars, exempt from federal estate, gift and generation-skipping transfer taxes, which your children and future generations could enjoy forever, you'd probably ask, "What's the catch?" There is no catch. And surprisingly enough, this little-known estate-planning technique, known today as a Dynasty Trust™, has been used for years by wealthy families.

It has been commonplace in America for affluent families to use trusts to transfer wealth to future generations. For years, the wealthy have used Dynasty Trusts™ to leave legacies for their children and successive generations. Many of these trusts, created at the turn of the century, still exist today. The original Dynasty Trusts™ were designed to pass as much wealth to future generations as possible while minimizing future federal estate taxes. In the past, vast amounts were placed into trusts to avoid the debilitating effects of estate taxes. Unfortunately, for today's families, the unique opportunities of the past have been limited by federal law. But resourceful estate-planning attorneys have found ways to utilize federal exemptions to modernize Dynasty Trusts™.

GENERATION-SKIPPING TRANSFER TRUSTS

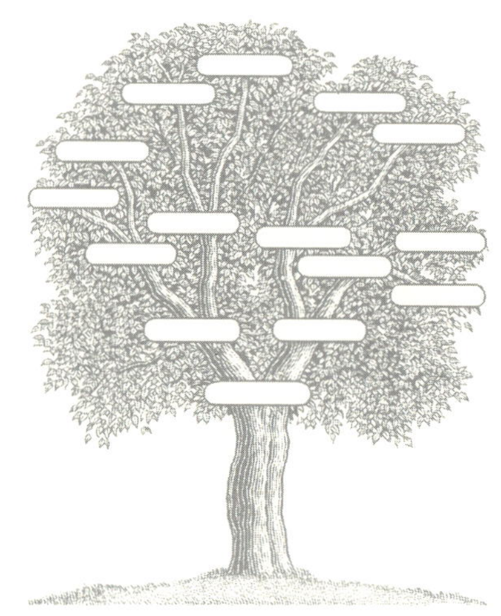

It is no revelation to say the federal government is fond of levying taxes. This has been especially true in the area of estate taxation. Assets passed to successive generations, either during someone's lifetime or at death, can be subject to estate, gift and generation-skipping transfer taxes. In the past, it was common practice for people to leave large legacies to grandchildren or great-grandchildren. By purposefully skipping generations, taxes could be put on hold or eliminated altogether.

In 1986, Congress passed legislation to deter this practice and assure the collection of taxes for transfers made either at death (testamentary) or during life (inter vivos) to generations at least twice removed from the person making the transfer; i.e., grandmother to granddaughter. The federal estate tax was substantially amended in the 2001 tax changes.[8]

---

[8]A complete discussion of the federal estate and gift tax system is beyond the scope of this chapter.

How a Modern Dynasty Trust™ Works

A Dynasty Trust™ is an irrevocable trust created for the benefit of the trustor's descendants and designed to exist as long as allowed by law, while utilizing part or all of the trustor's GSTT and other federal tax exemptions.

In most states a trust can only exist for about 100 years because of the common law "rule against perpetuities." A select few states[9] have abolished this rule, which means a Dynasty Trust™ with a situs (legal location) in one of these states can literally exist forever.

A Dynasty Trust™ can be created by placing assets into the trust during a person's lifetime or at death. An inter vivos (during life) Dynasty Trust™ has a distinct advantage over a testamentary Dynasty Trust™ because once assets are transferred into the trust and gift taxes paid, any further appreciation of assets or accumulated income is not subject to federal estate taxation for as long as the trust exists. Many estate planners favor an inter vivos Dynasty Trust™ believing it is more beneficial than a testamentary (at death) Dynasty Trust™, but each case is unique and must be approached on an individual basis.

Who Retains Control Over Trust Assets?

One of the primary goals of dynastic planning is elimination of federal taxes. Accomplishing this goal occurs when a trustor (maker) allocates part or all of his federal tax exemptions to the trust and he relinquishes all right, title and possession to trust assets. The trustor of a Dynasty Trust™ cannot retain a reversionary interest in the property in trust and cannot change the designated beneficiaries of the trust once it becomes irrevocable. Typically, the trustor cannot

[9]Alaska, Arizona, Delaware, Idaho, Illinois, Maryland, South Dakota and Wisconsin (1999). More states considering changes.

Discover how you can establish a multi-generation trust to share your blessings with the people you cherish.

"A good man leaves an inheritance for his children's children, but a sinner's wealth is stored up for the righteous."

Proverbs 13:22

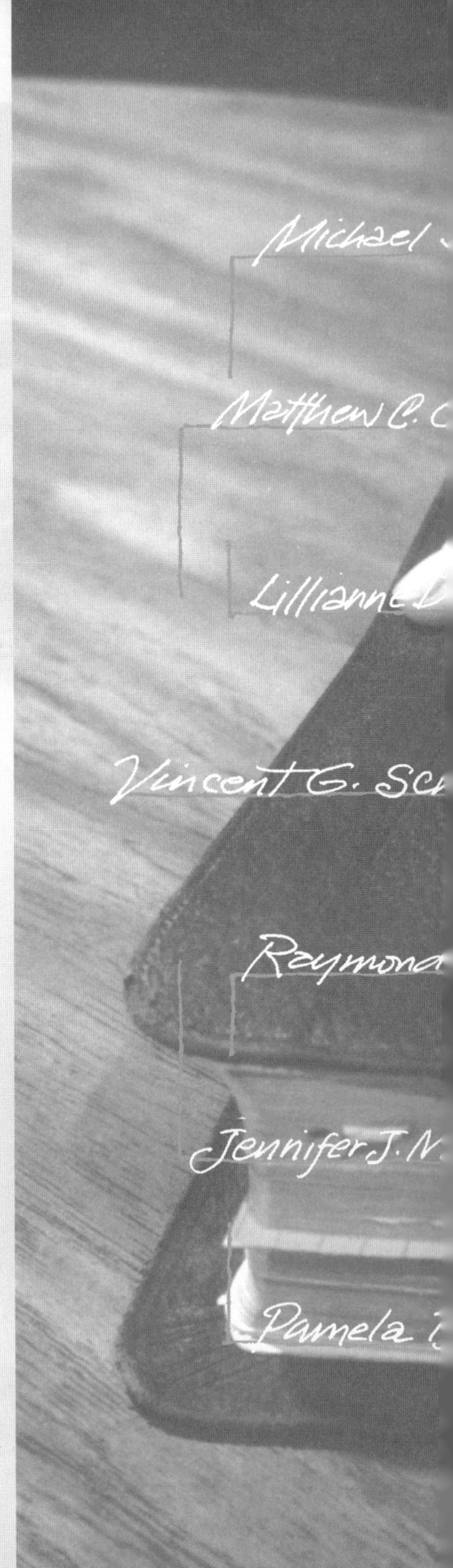

Preston S. Waldo

David B. Zangger

Shawn R. Orth

gh

Robert R. Uzzum

Brittany C. Koehler

Mary P. Roth

Richard B. Raunc

ason J. Peters

Melissa E. Curling

John S. Moyer

Susan C. Willaimson

Carol B. Vick

Scott T. Mundt

Curtis E. Edwards

Brook A. Tibbs

er

Martin R. Lightfoot

Carrie B. Davis

Judy D. Johnson

Jeffery S. Illies

Brent P. Boone

Catherine S. Haller

Eric J. Haccou

Cynthia A. Egan

Gina S. Alder

act as the trustee of the trust. Giving away the aforementioned powers allows the trust to exist free of federal estate taxation for as long as the trust exists. The trustor of a Dynasty Trust™ must have a sincere desire to transfer a selected portion of wealth indefinitely to future generations and must be willing to relinquish all control over certain assets.

Control of trust assets can be bestowed upon institutional trustees or private family trustees or a combination of both. Considering the complexity and magnitude of a Dynasty Trust™, an institutional

Trust Protector Statutes provide flexibility for a Dynasty Trust™ in an ever changing tax law environment.

trustee is recommended at least for administrative purposes.

Even though Dynasty Trusts™ are irrevocable, it does not mean the document is carved in stone for all eternity. Trust Protector Statutes allow the trustor to appoint a disinterested third party to act as Trust Protector. It is the Trust Protector's job to amend the trust, if changes in tax or other laws could adversely affect the trust. Having a Trust Protector provides flexibility for a Dynasty Trust™ in an ever changing tax law environment.

The Dynasty Trust™ can also provide for independent investment advice. If the family trustee or beneficiaries choose, an investment advisor for the trust can be hired to manage trust assets to further handle investment and financial responsibilities from family or institutional trustees. Having an investment advisor can greatly enhance a trust's portfolio and offer comfort to trustees and beneficiaries alike.

Who are the Beneficiaries of the Trust?

A Dynasty Trust™ is intended to benefit all of the trustor's lineal descendants for as long as the trust exists. If no lineal descendants exist, the trust can be structured to terminate and the contents given to charitable organizations.

How do the Beneficiaries Benefit From the Trust?

The trustor decides. A Dynasty Trust™ can either distribute or accumulate earned income depending on the trustor's goals and objectives. Distributions of income need not be equal amongst the beneficiary pool, and distributions can be made contingent upon an event (i.e., for every two dollars the beneficiary earns at his job, the trust will distribute $1 of income to him). In the illustration at right, *Example 1* shows how a $2 million estate can be preserved through a combination of a Dynasty Trust™ and life insurance.

This illustration assumes Husband and Wife are 55, in good health and non-tobacco risks. It utilizes a universal life policy at 6% interest with coverage enforced until age 100. *Example 2* depicts a single trustor who is 55, in good health and with non-tobacco risks, using a universal life policy; 6% interest.

WHERE SHOULD THE TRUSTOR ESTABLISH A DYNASTY TRUST™?

Where a trust is located, or its situs, is the most important decision the trustor has to make because situs selection can affect not only the duration of the Dynasty Trust™, but also income tax implications. It is recommended placing a Dynasty Trust™ in a state without a rule against perpetuities; but a more in-depth analysis of state income tax, state capital gains tax, state corporate tax, state intangibles tax and other applicable law should be considered before a situs is chosen. An attorney should be consulted before deciding where to establish a Dynasty Trust™.

ARE ASSETS HELD IN TRUST PROTECTED FROM CREDITORS?

Since Dynasty Trusts™ are irrevocable and the trustor has no retained rights in the assets, a trustor's creditors cannot lay claim to the assets. This is not the case for beneficiaries unless spendthrift provisions are incorporated into the trust. A spendthrift provision keeps a beneficiary's credit, marital or other financial problems from attaching the beneficiary's interest in the trust until after a distribu-

How Dynasty Trusts™ Work

Example 1:

$2 Million Estate

Husband and Wife create inter vivos Dynasty Trust™

↓

Dynasty Trust™ funded with up to $2 million.

↓

Assets used for a lump-sum purchase of a second-to-die policy on the lives of Husband and Wife.

↓

Second-to-die *policy worth approximately $30 million purchased (based on $2 million purchase).* Dynasty Trust™ *named beneficiary.*

↓

When surviving spouse dies, trust receives $30 million and family benefits from the proceeds for future generations.

Example 2:

$2 Million Estate

Trustor creates inter vivos *Dynasty Trust™.*

↓

Dynasty Trust™ funded with up to $1 million.

↓

Assets used for a lump-sum purchase of a policy on Trustor's life.

↓

Policy worth approximately $10 million purchased (based on $1 million purchase). Dynasty Trust™ named beneficiary.

↓

When trustor dies, trust receives $10 million and heirs benefit from the proceeds for future generations.

tion is made. Spendthrift provisions provide necessary protection for Dynasty Trusts™ and should be included in every trust when allowed by applicable law.

SUMMARY

Dynasty Trusts™ are obviously not for everyone. However, more and more families are finding use of these a beneficial tool in estate planning.

One popular trend to fund Dynasty Trusts™ has been to purchase last-to-die insurance on couples which, properly drafted and operated, can create tax-free income for beneficiaries for many years as long as there are heirs. A church and/or Christian organization can be named as an ultimate beneficiary or even an annual beneficiary in a Dynasty Trust™.

These are very complex trusts which can be extremely helpful in estate planning if properly drafted. It is important to know that there are tools available to accomplish whatever goals a person ultimately determines for disbursement of his worldly estate.

Put not
your trust
in money,
but your
money in
trust.

— Oliver Wendell Holmes

Call ~ Compare Attorneys

Who should be the Personal Representative or Executor of a Will?

WHAT IS AN IRREVOCABLE TRUST?

What is the difference between a "DURABLE POWER OF ATTORNEY" and a general "POWER OF ATTORNEY?"

?

WHAT DOES PROBATE COST?

How often should I review my ESTATE PLAN?

When will life insurance be included in my taxable estate?

GROCERIES:
butter
Turkey breast
Vanilla yogurt
alfalfa sprouts
green olives

How can heirs be kept from FIGHTING over Estates?

What is the difference between having a Durable Power of Attorney and having someone appointed as guardian?

What does it mean if property is held in joint tenancy?

Ask Questions!

What is a Codicil?

REMEMBER-
Dentist appt 10:30
soccer game 4:15
Hair Salon-SAT@9
ully's for dinner on Fri.

WHAT ARE SOME WAYS TO SPECIFY DIVISION OF PERSONAL EFFECTS ?

?

How can high costs of probate be avoided?

What is a Hamilton trust?

Can I disinherit my spouse or my children?

Who should be part of my ESTATE PLANNING "team?"

What is a "Durable Power of Attorney?"

How much can I give, tax free, to my children, spouse or any other person each year?

Can "probate" be avoided by a Living Trust?

?

?

What is a "POUR OVER" Will?

Can I put my children's names on certificates of deposit, real property, and other property in or... escape probate"

TAKE CHICKEN OUT OF FREEZER

What happens if I don't have a Will?

What is the difference between a "Living Trust" and a "Living Will?"

Can I give my property to the children and get government funds for nursing home care?

25 FREQUENTLY ASKED QUESTIONS ABOUT ESTATE PLANNING

Solutions

"For the Lord gives wisdom, and from his mouth come knowledge and understanding. He holds victory in store for the upright, ..."
— Proverbs 2:6-7

CHAPTER 14

There are no dumb questions. A question by its very nature is an unknown fact to be learned by those wise enough to seek an answer. No one should ever be labeled a dummy. Wise people seek answers to their questions. Every reader learns something and becomes smarter. Likewise, every person who asks questions becomes a more informed person.

It is said there are three ways we learn during our lives: by the books we read, the experiences we have and the people we encounter. By having access to helpful books, seeking positive experiences and searching for uplifting people, we can all learn.

We can enrich our lives by being "questioners" and "life long learners" each day allowing God to fill our lives with knowledge.

Many times people feel inadequate in dealing with professionals therefore failing to ask questions. It is really a form of self-intimidation. Jotting down questions before visiting any professional ... doctor ... lawyer ... insurance agent ... financial planner ... can be a helpful tool in being sure every question is answered. And any competent, caring professional welcomes questions.

Returning for a moment to the "Pyramid of Risks" in conversation, there is little risk in asking questions. There should be no feeling of rejection in receiving an answer.

Law presents its own problems for understanding personal choices. Too often, law gets tangled, mangled and strangled in the mass of "lawyer language" — commas, periods, Latin and frankly that which sounds like Greek to most people. In fact, lawyers get accused of coding their professional talk in such a way that another lawyer needs to be hired to explain the code. That is not true, but that is the perception.

This is an attempt to take the most common questions people ask about estate planning and offer simple answers.

1 What is the difference between a "Living Trust" and a "Living Will?"

Because federal law requires a "health directive" be presented as an option before entering a medical facility, "Living Wills" have received lots of publicity. Living Wills address terminal health care issues and generally direct physicians as to whether life-sustaining treatment should be withheld, continued or modified in a variety of life-ending situations.

A regular Will addresses disposition of property after death. A Living Will only addresses the medical response to terminating life support. They are generally separate documents.

Separate from both of these are so-called Living Trusts. They have been popularly marketed as probate-avoiding documents. These are nothing more than revocable trusts. A donor puts the property in trust. It is managed under terms of the trust and upon the passing of the maker of the trust, the property is transferred to the designated beneficiary. These have a variety of names but all have the same legal roots.

2 Can "probate" be avoided by a Living Trust?

Probate is a very general legal term defining the disposition of assets after death. A Living Trust may not completely eliminate probate, but it has many administrative benefits. A state inheritance tax report must still be filed on property in a Living Trust in states requiring this. Any property not included in the trust at the time of death must still be "probated." On larger estates, there may be a federal estate tax return to complete. While a Living Trust can streamline estate administration, it is not a cure-all for handling estates or avoiding probate.

3 What is a "Durable Power of Attorney?"

This is a document wherein you give the power to someone else (such as a spouse or offspring) to make all financial decisions and execute documents for you in the event you are unable to do so, even beyond competency. If health powers are included, the person holding the Durable Power of Attorney can make health decisions along with financial decisions on your behalf.

The Question is NOT "what can God do for you?"
BUT, "What can You do for God?"
roclaiming the Word and Witness of Jesus Christ?

What happens if I don't have a Will?

Everyone has a Will. Either you have a written one or your state legislature has written one for you.

The law of intestate succession (dying without a Will) for your state spells out in law what happens to your property if you have not written your own Will.

> **"Everyone has a Will ... written either by you or the state."**

5 How can high costs of probate be avoided?

A good estate plan is your best defense. Obtaining in writing attorney fees to be charged is a very important step. All other costs can be estimated as a part of an estate plan.

Even on small estates, disposition of property can become costly if the heirs fight over ambiguous parts of the estate, or if there are property title problems which could have been avoided by well-drafted estate documents.

How can heirs be kept from fighting over estates?

Usually estate fights develop over a poorly drawn Will where the intentions are not clear or where there is no Will.

Most of the time family feuds develop over "personal effects." Most Wills will say to divide personal property "equally" amongst the heirs. But "equally" is hard to define between two daughters wanting Mom's wedding ring.

A well-drawn Will specifying a formula for division of personal property and personal effects, which represents the intention of the person making the Will, is important. This is normally unchallenged and can avoid fights.

What are some ways to specify division of personal effects?

There are five major ways to dispose of "personal effects" in a Will with variations of these that can be developed:

- Do nothing. Let the heirs and personal representatives or court define a formula of dividing everything "equally."
- Specify by item who is to get what in the Will or attach a properly drafted exhibit to the Will.
- Order the personal property divided into equal units and then by lot draw for the various units.
- Random selection with either a drawing deciding who picks first or a preset order such as the oldest to youngest child with each picking items in rotation until all property is dispersed.
- Auction off all personal effects with heirs having a right to bid.

Who should be the Personal Representative or Executor of a Will?

The person you trust most who is able to handle the disposition of your affairs is the right choice.

9 Can I give my property to the children and get government funds for nursing home care?

Probably not under today's strict rules and laws. With new government regulations, persons having assets are required to use those assets if they need nursing home care. In 1993 a three- to five-year "look back" rule was implemented depending on the program and circumstances. This means property transferred within the time of needing government assistance can be voided.

The government does not force the sale of property or take it for nursing home care. They deny benefits to persons having assets or wrongfully transferring assets. This, in effect, can force the sale of family assets.

There are stiff penalties for attempting to defraud the government by asset transfers to children or relatives. However, if one spouse goes into a nursing home, a homestead exemption is part of this formula, so the other spouse can retain adequate property and income. This is a very complicated formula and should be discussed on a case-by-case basis as a part of a pre-estate plan.

For persons having some assets, a long-term-care insurance policy may be a better option than some false belief the government will pay nursing home costs.

10 Can I put my children's names on certificates of deposit, real property, and other property in order to escape probate?

The use of this type of estate planning with a power of attorney and other patchwork attempts to work through the maze of estate laws is probably the most costly and risky method of estate planning.

Since you have worked all your life for what you have, perhaps spending a few hours to properly plan the disposition of your property as you choose is the best investment you can make.

11 What is the difference between a Will and a Living Trust?

A Will is your final direction for the disposition of your property. It is handled by naming a personal representative or executor to complete all work in finalizing your estate.

A Living Trust is a revocable trust in which you have put your assets. Instead of an executor, you have a trustee. This may be a family member, friend or institutional trust. The trustee distributes your property, pays all expenses and taxes, and handles all final distribution of your estate.

12 What does probate cost?

Probate costs can vary due to the size and complexity of an estate. Some attorneys charge a percentage of the gross estate and others by an hourly rate. A growing trend is a negotiated "fixed fee" which reduces the cost of probate. The fee is set unless there are extraordinary circumstances that appear during probate such as a court fight over property. Getting the fee in writing from the attorney before hiring counsel for a probate is the best way to eliminate problems over probate costs.

In states having the informal probate laws under the Uniform Probate Code, the cost of probate is on average much less because court appearances are rarely needed to complete an estate.

The purpose of research is to find the facts, analyze the facts, and act upon the facts.

13 What is a "pour over" Will?

This is a Will recommended for persons having a Living Trust which states that if there is any property at death that is not in the Living Trust, the Will pours the property into the trust. For example, unknown assets of an estate can develop even after a death, such as an unexpected family inheritance, or if death is caused by an accident there may be a "wrongful death claim." These proceeds could be distributed through a Living Trust if there is a companion "pour over" Will.

What does it mean if property is held in joint tenancy?

Property held in joint tenancy means the party who lives the longest will get the property. Property listed in joint tenancy supersedes how property is distributed in a Will. So if a home is owned in joint tenancy with a spouse and a wife survives her husband, the house will go to her. This can happen even if the Will says part of the house proceeds should go to children. Any future distribution of the house sale proceeds will be governed by her Will, and her Will could be changed at any time.

15 What is an irrevocable trust?

By definition, this is a trust that usually cannot be changed once the terms and conditions are written. Though the provisions of an irrevocable trust can have numerous options depending on a variety of events, once property is placed in an irrevocable trust it is a near legal impossibility to change what will happen to that property.

If an irrevocable trust is used to avoid creditors or wrongfully obtain government payments, it can be attacked. So like most legal matters, using the word "never" is not always accurate. And there are some states which give trustees legal power to reform or change irrevocable trusts in limited circumstances.

16 What is a Hamilton trust?

A Hamilton trust is a special trust set up for heirs having special needs. Usually these are set up so a disabled heir can legally continue obtaining government benefits and enjoy his share of an estate for "life enhancement" rather than basic needs. In most of these cases, upon the demise of the special-needs heir, the portion in the Hamilton trust is then given to other surviving heirs of the family.

Special needs children can have their inheritance protected.

17 How much can I give, tax free, to my children, spouse or any other person each year?

Each person can give another up to $10,000 per year without paying federal gift tax under current law. A husband and wife, for example, can each give each child $10,000 per year or a total of $20,000 per child. There are no age limits on this. This has become an important tool to minimize federal estate taxes and to stop the growth of estates that could end up paying substantial federal estate taxes. Spouses can transfer unlimited amounts between each other without federal tax consequences as long as they are both alive.

18 When will life insurance be included in my taxable estate?

Life insurance will be included in a taxable estate: A) if the proceeds are payable to or for the benefit of the insured's estate, B) if the insured has any "incidents of ownership" in the policy when he or she died (i.e., right to change beneficiaries, right to borrow against the policy), or C) if the insured transferred ownership rights in the policy to another person or a legal entity within three years of death.

19 What is a holographic Will?

This is a Will physically written in one's own hand with clear intentions, signed and dated. It is legal in some but not in all states. Frequently, these Wills are called "homemade Wills." They can be just as legal as those drawn by an attorney but a higher percentage end up in litigation because of the strict legal requirements for having such a Will admitted to probate.

20 What is a codicil?

This is nothing more than a fancy legal word for an "amendment" or change of an original Will. It is signed and witnessed the same way a Will is signed and witnessed but not necessarily by the same witnesses.

21 What is the difference between having a Durable Power of Attorney and having someone appointed as guardian?

A guardianship is court supervision over a living person who cannot take care of himself or his affairs. A Durable Power of Attorney gives similar powers to another person without court supervision. It is a powerful document as the maker is literally allowing another person to stand in his shoes and do everything he would do if he could physically or mentally do so. There are far more safeguards in a guardianship than a Durable Power of Attorney.

What is the difference between a "Durable Power of Attorney" and a general "Power of Attorney?"

A Durable Power of Attorney survives competency of an individual in addition to all other powers that are normally in a general power of attorney. Both terminate upon the death of the maker of the document.

Who stands in your shoes?

23 Can I disinherit my spouse or my children?

Disinheriting a spouse is far more difficult than disinheriting a child. Most states have statutes providing that spouses get a certain percentage or flat sum of an estate regardless of what is in the Will. This is called the "spouses elective share" among other terms. The spouse has to assert this as a claim on the estate; the laws vary greatly by state. Generally, a prenuptial agreement between the parties will address this issue. In the case of "blended families," this is becoming a greater issue.

If the laws are followed, children can be disinherited, although in most states that cannot be done for a minor or disabled child. Again, these laws vary from state to state and need the guidance of a competent estate planning attorney.

24 How often should I review my estate plan?

Anytime there is a change in family circumstances or law, your estate plan should be reviewed. Just as you review insurance coverage and other financial matters regularly, your estate plan should be reviewed. Having worked all your life for what you have, spending an hour or so each year reviewing all estate planning documents is good stewardship and good business.

Who should be part of my estate planning "team"?

The most important decision regarding who is on your team is to have people you trust. Many times a CPA or tax preparer is involved. Life insurance agents are major contributors to most estate-planning packages. Stockbrokers and financial planners have become an integral part of many estate planning teams.

It is suggested key family members, certainly designated executors, personal representatives or trustees, be involved. An attorney who practices estate planning is worth far more than the legal fees in crafting a plan that truly reflects your "will."

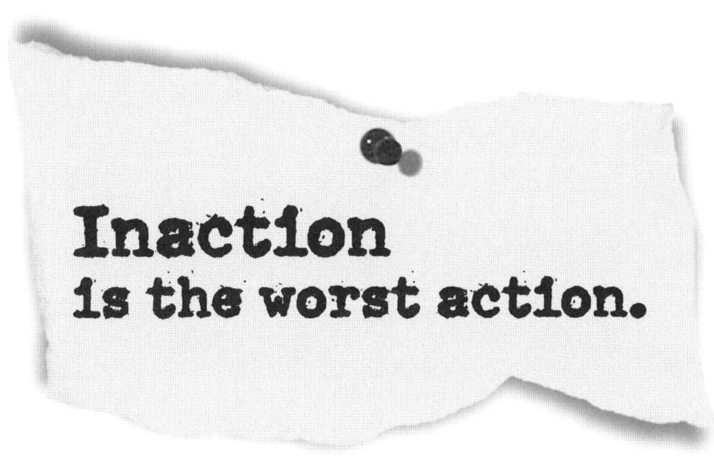

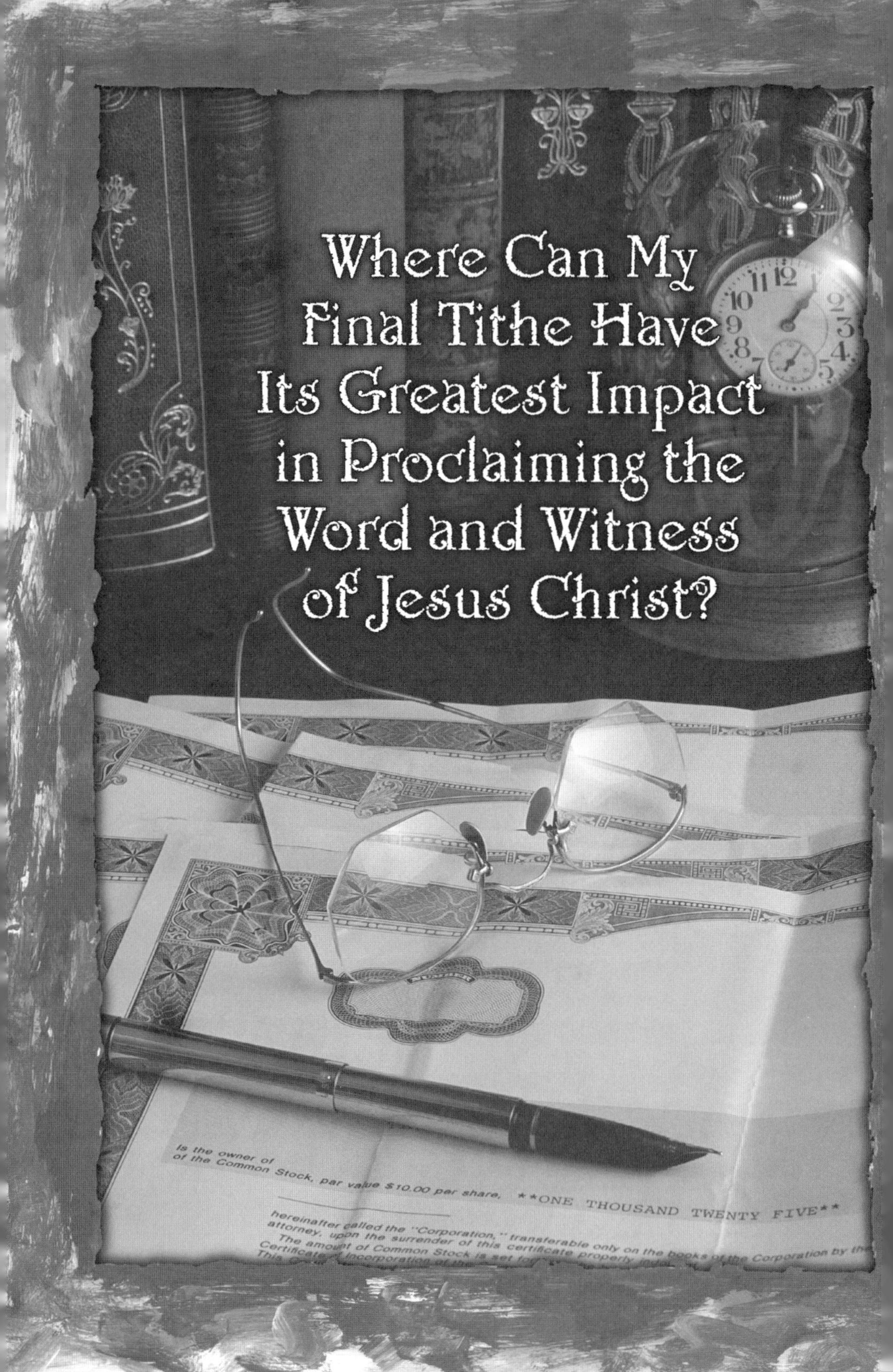
Where Can My
Final Tithe Have
Its Greatest Impact
in Proclaiming the
Word and Witness
of Jesus Christ?
Is the owner of
of the Common Stock, par value $10.00 per share, **ONE THOUSAND TWENTY FIVE**
hereinafter called the "Corporation," transferable only on the books of the Corporation by the
attorney, upon the surrender of this certificate properly

HOW TO REMEMBER YOUR CHURCH AND CHRISTIAN ORGANIZATIONS BY YOUR FINAL TITHE

Vision

"The time has come," he said. "The kingdom of God is near. Repent and believe the good news!"
— Mark 1:15.

CHAPTER 15

Including a paragraph in your Will reflecting your final tithe, based on the examples in this book, is sufficient to make your gift to your church and/or favorite Christian organization. For your local church, all you need to obtain is the legal name and address of the church for inclusion in your Will.

For leading national Christian organizations, the legal titles of contact and legal name of these organizations is provided alphabetically in this chapter. This is not a comprehensive list of every national or international Christian organization but a selection of some of the leading organizations that carry out the work of Jesus Christ. Any of these organizations can be named in your Will, and the appropriate amounts will be provided them by your estate.

There are also numerous Christian schools, colleges and seminaries that have endowments. They accept gifts by Wills, trusts or other estate-planning devices including life insurance policies. To get the proper name of a Christian school, college or seminary for inclusion in your Will, a contact from you or your attorney to the development office of any of these institutions will provide the proper legal name for inclusion in your final gift.

Most of these organizations have active programs for donations through estates. Their literature is generally excellent and informative. Obtaining copies can provide gifting options for you to consider as a part of your "final tithe."

Many Christians are concerned that their gifts to various church-related organizations be properly managed. One of the sources of accountability is the Evangelical Council for Financial Accountability. Their standards and the organizations reporting to them are among the highest for any Christian organization.

Here is a summary of this organization's work to help Christians make their giving decisions.

STEWARDSHIP

EVANGELICAL COUNCIL FOR FINANCIAL ACCOUNTABILITY
Standards of Responsible Stewardship for Members

Standard #1 Doctrinal Statement

Every member organization shall subscribe to a written statement of faith clearly affirming its commitment to the evangelical Christian faith and shall conduct its financial operations in a manner which reflects those generally accepted biblical truths and practices.

Standard #2 Board of Directors and Audit Review Committee

Every member organization shall be governed by a responsible board of not less than five individuals, a majority of whom shall be other than employees/staff and/or those related by blood or marriage, which shall meet at least semi-annually to establish policy and review its accomplishments. The board shall appoint a functioning audit review committee, a majority of whom shall be other than employees/staff and/or those related by blood or marriage, for the purpose of reviewing the annual audit and reporting its findings to the board.

Standard #3 Audited Financial Statements

Every member organization shall obtain an annual audit performed by an independent public accounting firm in accordance with Generally Accepted Auditing Standards (GAAS) with financial statements prepared in accordance with Generally Accepted Accounting Principals (GAAP).

Standard #4 Controls for Transferring Contributions

Every member organization shall exercise management and financial controls necessary to provide reasonable assurance that all resources are used (nationally and internationally) to accomplish the exempt purposes for which they are intended.

Standard #5 Financial Disclosure

Every member organization shall provide a copy of its current audited financial statements upon written request.

Standard #6 Conflicts of Interest

Every member organization shall avoid conflicts of interest. Transactions with related parties may be undertaken only if all of the following are observed: 1) a material transaction is fully disclosed in the audited financial statements of the organization; 2) the related party is excluded from the discussion and approval of such transaction; 3) a competitive bid or comparable valuation exists; and 4) the organization's board has acted upon and demonstrated that the transaction is in the best interests of the member organization.

Standard #7 Fund Raising

Every member organization shall comply with each of the ECFA Standards for Fund Raising:

7.1 Truthfulness in Communication: All representations of fact, description of financial condition of the organization, or narrative about events must be current, complete and accurate. There may be no material omissions or exaggerations of fact or use of misleading photographs or any other communication which would tend to create a false impression or misunderstanding.

7.2 Communication and Donor Expectations: Fund-raising appeals must not create unrealistic donor expectations of what a donor's gift will actually accomplish within the limits of the organization's ministry.

7.3 Communication and Donor Intent: All statements made by an organization in its fund-raising appeals about the use of the gift must be honored by the organization. The donor's intent is related to both what was communicated in the appeal and to any donor instructions accompanying the gift. Organizations should be aware that communications made in fund-raising appeals may create a legally binding restriction.

7.4 Projects Unrelated to a Ministry's Primary Purpose: When an organization raises or receives funds for programs that are not part of its present or prospective ministry, it should either treat them as restricted funds and channel them through an organization that can carry out the donor's intent or return the funds to the donor.

7.5 Incentives and Premiums: When appeals for funds offer premiums or incentives, the value of which is significant in relation to the amount of the donation, the donor should be advised of any non-deductible value of the premium or incentive for tax purposes.

7.6 Reporting: If requested, an organization must provide a report on the project for which it is soliciting gifts.

7.7 Risk Capital and Fund Raising: Use of risk capital to finance a fund-raising project is specifically prohibited where return or compensation is tied directly or indirectly to the amount of income derived from tax-deductible gifts to the project.

7.8 Percentage Compensation for Fund Raisers: Compensation of anyone involved in the fund-raising process may not be based directly or indirectly on a percentage of what is raised or on any other contingency agreement.

7.9 Tax-Deductible Gifts for a Named Recipient's Personal Benefit: Tax-deductible gifts may not be used to pass money or benefits to any named individual for personal use, or to pay tuition or other expenses which should be a personal expense (i.e. expenses not included in the authorized salary budgeted account of the applicable ministry or project).

7.10 Conflict of Interest on Royalties: Avoid conflicts of interest by non-paying royalties for a copyrighted product to officer, director, or other principal of the organization in instances where that product is used for fund raising and/or promotional purposes by the nonprofit organization.

7.11 Acknowledgment of Gifts in Kind: When property or gifts in kind are received by an organization, the acknowledgment should describe the property or gift accurately without a statement of the gift's market value. It is the responsibility of the donor to determine the fair market value of the property for tax purposes.

7.12 Percentage of Overall Fund-Raising Costs in Comparing Christian Organizations: Percentage guidelines for fund-raising costs cannot be used as standards to

compare one organization to another because costs must be evaluated separately for each organization according to the following variants:

- Length of donor cultivation;
- Cost of name or donor acquisition;
- Different allocation methods for determining program, management, and fund-raising costs;
- Existence of low-cost fund-raising activities by some organizations.

7.13 Acting in the Interests of the Donor: In dealing with prospective deferred gift donors, every effort must be made to avoid accepting a gift or entering into a contract which would knowingly place a hardship on the donor or place the donor's future well-being in jeopardy.

7.14 Financial Advice: When dealing with persons regarding commitments on major estate assets, the representative of the organization must seek to guide and advise donors so they have adequately considered the broad interests of the family and the various ministries they are currently supporting before they make a final decision. Donors should be encouraged to use the services of their attorneys or accountants. If any of these standards are not in keeping with legal or accounting requirements in countries other than the United States, it is understood that the governmental and accounting requirements in these countries take precedent.

For more information contact:

Paul Nelson, President
Evangelical Center for Financial Accountability
P. O. Box 17456, Washington, DC 20041-0456
Telephone: 800-323-9473
email: ecfa@aol.com

FREQUENTLY ASKED QUESTIONS ABOUT ECFA

Who are the members of the ECFA?

ECFA members are evangelical Christian nonprofit organizations that have demonstrated compliance with the ECFA Seven Standards of Responsible Stewardship. ECFA members are all recognized by the IRS as tax-exempt organizations as described in section 501(c)(3) of the Internal Revenue Code.

How can I determine if a particular ministry is a member of ECFA?

You may search through our Member Directory on our web site; or you may contact ECFA by telephone at 800-3BE-WISE (800-323-9473), by email at webmaster@ecfa.org, or by writing ECFA, P. O. Box 17456, Washington, DC 20041-0456. ECFA publishes a member list at least once per year and provides a member profile on individual ECFA members, which provides additional details on specific ECFA members.

Are organizations that are not members of ECFA to be considered unethical or unworthy of financial support?

No. ECFA membership is voluntary and there may be various reasons why an organization may not choose to become a member of ECFA. Many organizations may not subscribe to the evangelical Christian statement of faith. Some organizations are too small to justify the cost of an annual audit (a requirement for membership). There are others that may not have a board governance structure that conforms to ECFA standards.

The organizations that are members of ECFA have voluntarily chosen to use ECFA as a tangible means of demonstrating accountability and excellence. They have submitted themselves to the scrutiny of ECFA in their desire to operate in keeping with the scriptural principles of 2 Corinthians 8:21 (NIV): *"For we are taking pains to do what is right, not only in the eyes of the Lord, but also in the eyes of men."*

ECFA has published a Giver's Guide, which is intended to help donors know what to look for and what questions to ask before giving to any charity, whether it is an ECFA member or not. The Giver's Guide includes a "Donor's Bill of Rights" which details the information to which ECFA believes donors are entitled.

How often does ECFA review each member organization to be sure it maintains compliance with ECFA standards?

ECFA evaluates all of its members annually through a procedure called the Annual Membership Review. Members are asked to submit documentation which supports their continued compliance with the standards. This documentation includes in part:

- Recent audited financial statements;
- A list of current Board members and Audit Review Committee Members;
- Samples of fund-raising appeals;
- Annual Report;
- Salaries and remuneration of top five paid employees;
- Completed questionnaire, signed by the member's Chief Executive Officer, Chief Financial Officer and Chairman of the Board.

ECFA also performs a field review on approximately 30 to 40 randomly selected members each year. The field review is conducted at the member organization's headquarters, and ECFA representatives conduct interviews with the organization's management, board chairman, audit review chairman and auditor. The field review is intended to reinforce and confirm the reporting made by the member organization in its annual membership review.

When complaints about members are received, a compliance review is conducted on the member(s) in question. The compliance review is intended to investigate allegations of non-compliance with ECFA standards. Depending on the seriousness of the concern, the compliance review may also involve an on-site evaluation of the member.

Which organizations in your membership are the most efficient in terms of the percentage of donated money actually being spent on ministry objectives rather than fund raising or overhead?

ECFA does not rank its members according to percentages. There are many variables that may affect the percentages, including the age and size of the organization, the popularity of its purposes, differences in accounting procedures, etc. ECFA has tried to dispel the myth that organizations with a low percentage of fund raising and overhead are more efficient or effective than those with higher percentages of fund raising and overhead costs. Contact the ECFA office for more information on this subject.

Who is the best ECFA member organization to support?

Again, ECFA does not rank its members. All members must consistently demonstrate compliance with all ECFA standards in order to be a member of ECFA in good standing. Noncompliance with any one standard is grounds for dismissal from membership.

Where can I make my final tithe gift to advance the cause of our Lord?

ORGANIZATIONS AVAILABLE FOR FINAL TITHE GIFTS

How can I contact organizations I may wish to consider for making a final tithe?

The following is a list of various organizations the Fellowship of Christian Estate Planners, Inc. has considered for potential support, even though giving decisions must be made by individuals and their own financial advisors. This list is compiled for purposes of making contact and learning more about the long-term giving opportunities to these organizations and should not be considered an endorsement of any one.

Mr. Dick Innes, Director
ACTS International, U.S.A.
250 West Colorado Boulevard, Ste. 240
Arcadia, CA 91007
phone 949-940-9050
fax 949-481-3686
acts@actsweb.org
www.actsweb.org

Mr. Dan Lemmen, President
Adopt-A-Church International, Inc.
P. O. Box 510
Allendale, MI 49401-0510
phone 616-892-4260
www.adoptachurch.org
To establish relationships between churches and families in the West to provide spiritual, financial and moral support to the churches and pastors in Eastern Europe.

Mr. Ron Ovitt, Customer Service
Adventures in Missions
6000 Wellspring Trail
Gainsville, GA 30506
phone 770-983-1060
fax 770-983-1061
ronovitt@adventures.org
www.adventures.org
Short-term mission trips for young people and adults.

Mr. Samuel Ericsson, President
Advocates International
9691 D Main Street
Fairfax, VA 22031-3754
phone 703-764-0011
fax 703-764-0077
www.advocatesinternational.org
International religious liberty.

Mr. J. Douglas McDaniel
Planned Gift Programs
American Bible Society
1865 Broadway, 8th Floor
New York, NY 10023-7505
phone 212-408-1286
fax 212-408-1238
www.americanbiblesociety.org
Making the Bible available to every person in a language and format each can understand and afford.

Ms. Carol Masters, Director of Major Donor Development
American Leprosy Missions
One ALM Way
Greenville, SC 29601
phone 800-543-3135
fax 864-241-1755
amlep@leprosy.org
www.leprosy.org
Worldwide assistance to people affected by leprosy.

Mr. Gary Powell
Ministry Manager
American Scripture Gift Mission
P. O. Box 410280
Melbourne, FL 32941
phone 877-873-2746 or 321-255-7774
fax 321-255-8986
asgm@asgm.com
www.asgm.com
Distributing Scripture booklets in 400 languages.

Mr. Scott Wynant
Executive Vice President
Assemblies of God Foundation
1661 North Boonville Avenue, Suite D
Springfield, MO 65803-1894
phone 800-253-5544
fax 417-863-5141
Directing God-given resources to God-given goals.

Ms. Debbie R. Thomas
Executive Director
Assoc. of Camps Farthest Out, Inc.
317 South Madison Avenue
Watkins Glen, NY 14891-1120
phone 607-535-4415
fax 607-535-9689
info@campsfarthestout.org
www.campsfarthestout.org

Mr. Bryon Swanson
President
Back to the Bible Foundation
P. O. Box 82808
Lincoln, NE 68501-2808
phone 800-759-6655
fax 402-464-7219
foundation@backtothebible.org
www.stewardshipsolutions.org
To lead people into a dynamic relationship with God.

Baja Christian Ministries
4195 Chino Hills Parkway #390
Chino Hills, CA 91709
phone 909-627-4339
fax 909-627-1768
bajachrist@aol.com
www.bajachristian.org
Serving the poor in Baja Mexico through house building, outreach and church planting.

Mr. Lee Jantzen
Ministry Partner Services
Baptist General Conference
2002 S. Arlington Heights Road
Arlington Heights, IL 60005
phone 847-228-0200
fax 847-228-5376
ljantzen@baptistgeneral.org
www.bgcworld.org
Church planting and church enrichment.

Keith Meyering
CFRE, Director of Planned Giving
Bethany Christian Service
P. O. Box 294
Grand Rapids, MI 49501-0294
phone 616-224-7431
fax 616-224-7432
kmeyering@bethany.org
www.bethany.org
To provide quality Christian social services at home and abroad.

Billy Graham Evangelistic Assoc.
1 Billy Graham Parkway
Charlotte, NC 28201-0001
phone 704-401-2432
www.billygraham.org
Evangelism.

Mr. Stephen M. Davis
CPGE, Director of Estate and Gift Design
The Bible League
P.O. Box 28000
Chicago, IL 60628
phone 708-367-8528
fax 708-367-8924
sdavis@bibleleague.org
www.bibleleague.org
Providing God's word to bring people to Christ.

Ms. Diana Hunt
Director of Development
Bread for the World
50 F Street NW, No. 500
Washington, DC 20001
phone 800-82-BREAD
fax 202-639-9401

Ms. Kyle Becchetti
VP Operations
Center for Student Missions
P.O. Box 900
Dana Point, CA 92629-0900
phone 949-248-8200
fax 949-248-7753
csm@csm.org
www.csm.org
Links suburban/rural churches with inner-city ministries.

Terre K. Richie
Executive Director
Children's Bible Hour
Box 1
Grand Rapids, MI 49331
phone 616-647-4500
fax 616-647-4950
davec@cbhministries.org
www.cbhministries.org
Evangelism and discipleship of children through media.

Dr. Jonathan Chao
CMI United States
P. O. Box 40489
Pasadena, CA 91114-7489
phone 626-398-0145
fax 626-398-2361
cmius@csi; www.cmi.org.tw/
Protestant mission organization conducting research and training of pastors in China.

Ms. Roberta Josephson, Accountant
Christian Aid Mission
P. O. Box 9037
Charlottesville, VA 22906
phone 804-977-5650
fax 804-295-6814
ask@christianaid.org
www.christianaid.org
Helping indigenous evangelical missions to win souls, plant churches and assist the poor in every nation.

Christian Appalachian Project
Planned Giving Department
P.O. Box 511
Lancaster, KY 40444-0511
phone 866-270-4227 or 859-792-3051
fax 859-792-6560
yourlegacy@chrisapp.org
www.chrisapp.org
Human services.

Ms. Joanne Wood
Christian Blind Mission International
450 East Park Avenue
Greenville, SC 29601
phone 864-239-0065
fax 864-239-0069
jwood@cbmi-usa.org
Provide medical care, preventing and curing blindness, as well as the rehabilitation and training of disabled people.

Sr. Robert Finley
Director
Christian Aid Mission
P. O. Box 9037
Charlottesville, VA 22906
phone 804-977-5650

Ms. Christie Williford
Planned Giving Department
The Christian Broadcasting Network
977 Centerville Turnpike
Virginia Beach, VA 23463
phone 757-226-7000

Mr. Robert L. Smythers
Planned Giving Manager
Christian Children's Fund
Box 26484
Richmond, VA 23261-5066
phone 804-756-2777
fax 804-756-2718
www.christianchildrensfund.org
Serving the health and education needs of poor children worldwide.

Ms. Rachel Pierson
Vice President of Fiscal Operations
Christian Church Foundation/ Handicapped
P. O. Box 9867
Knoxville, TN 37940
phone 865-546-5921
fax 865-525-2282
rpierson@ccfh.org
www.ccfh.org
Education, advocacy and residential placement for persons with disabilities.

Ms. Rita Bennett
President
Christian Renewal Association, Inc.
P. O. Box 576
Edmonds, WA 98020
phone 425-775-2965
fax 425-775-2033
www.emotionallyfree.org
To bring emotional and spiritual healing to those in need regardless of race or creed.

Mr. Bob Harding
Chief Financial Officer
Christian World Foundation
303 Seventh Avenue East
Hendersonville, NC 28792
phone 828-693-7007 ext. 308
fax 828-693-8113
hardingb@cwa.org
www.cwa.org
Placement, nutrition and medication for international children.

Ms. Teresa Waddle
Secretary, Planned/Major Giving
Church World Service
P. O. Box 968
Elkhart, IN 46515
phone 219-264-3102
fax 219-206-7880
www.churchworldservice.org
Disaster relief, self-help development, and refugee assistance.

Dr. Scott Walston, Director
Commission To Every Nation
815 Jefferson Street, Ste. 2000
Kerrville, TX 78028
phone 800-872-5404
fax 830-896-5262
scottwalston@cten.org
www.cten.org
National and International mission-sending agency helping missionaries fulfill their God-Given calling.

Mr. Lyndon R. Thompson
Supervisor, Christian Financial Planning
Kenneth Copeland Ministries
Fort Worth, TX 76192-0001
phone 817-252-2180
lthompson@kcm.org
www.kcm.org
International ministry.

Ms. Carolyn Koole
Director of Estate Planning
Cornerstone University
1001 East Beltline NE
Grand Rapids, MI 49525
phone 616-222-1539
fax 616-222-1414
carolyn_a_koole@cornerstone.edu
www.cornerstone.edu
Education.

Mr. Gordon Dornbush
Office Manager
Dynamic Youth Ministries
P.O. Box 7259
Grand Rapids, MI 49510
phone 616-241-5616 ext. 3022
fax 616-241-5558
gordon@dynamicyouthministries.org
www.dynamicyouthministries.org
Providing children and youth programming to the local church.

East Gates Ministries
P. O. Box 2010
Sumner, WA 98390
phone 253-770-2625
fax 253-770-2817
egmi@egmi.org
www.egmi.org
To help the body of Christ in China fulfill the Great Commission.

Mr. Mike Sullivan
Echo
17391 Durrance Road
North Ft. Myers, FL 33917
phone 239-543-3246
fax 239-543-5317
msullivan@echonet.org
www.echonet.org
Networking global hunger solutions.

Mr. Dave McCauley
Board Chair
Emmanuel International
3878 Concord Road
York, SC 29745
phone 803-831-1356
fax 803-831-1369
davemccauley@mindspring.com
Provide relief and development services working under the local national church in third-world countries.

Mr. Mark Petersburg
Vice President for Development
Enterprise Development International
10395-B Democracy Lane
Fairfax, VA 22030
phone 703-277-3360
enterprise@endpoverty.org
www.endpoverty.org
Microeconomic development among the poor.

Planned Giving Department
Every Home for Christ
P. O. Box 64000
Colorado Springs, CO 80962-4000
phone 800-423-5054
fax 719-260-7505
info@ehc.org
www.ehc.gift-planning.org
To pray for and personally present a printed or repeatable message of the Gospel of Jesus Christ to every home in the world.

Mr. Joseph Richter
Executive Director
FARMS International
P. O. Box 270
Knife River, MN 55609-0270
phone 218-834-2676
fax 218-834-2676
info@farmsintrenational.com
www.farmsinternational.com
Micro-credit for Christian families in poverty.

Mr. Jim Ray
Estate Planning Manager
Family Life Communications Inc.
P. O. Box 35300
Tucson, AZ 85740
phone 800-776-1070
fax 520-572-6979
jray@flc.org
www.flc.org
Religious broadcasting.

Mr. Bob Brown
Director of Planned Giving
Feed the Children
333 North Meridian Avenue
Oklahoma City, OK 73107-6568
phone 800-627-4556, fax 405-945-4198
bob.brown@feedthechildren.org.

Feeding Children International – Kids Against Hunger
5407 Boone Avenue North
New Hope, MN 55428
phone 763-257-0202
fax 763-504-2943
info@fedingchildren.org
www.feedingchildren.com
Feeding starving children in the United States and the world.

Mr. Dave Davies
Fellowship of Christian Athletes
8701 Leeds Road
Kansas City, MO 64129
phone 816-921-0909
fax 816-921-8755
ddavies@fca.org
To see the world impacted for Jesus Christ through the influence of athletes and coaches.

Food For The Hungry Foundation
Food for the Hungry
1224 E. Washington Street
Phoenix, AZ 85034
phone 800-248-6437
fax 480-998-4461
www.fh.org
Christian relief and development.

Foundation for His Ministry
P. O. Box 74000
San Clemente, CA 92673-0134
phone 949-492-2200
fax 949-492-0900
ffhm@juno.com
www.ffhm.org
Ministering to homeless children and the poorest of the poor.

Mr. Steve Anderson
Associate Executive Director
Girls and Boys Town (the original Father Flanagan's Boys Home)
300 Flanagan Boulevard,
P. O. Box 7000
Boys Town, NE 68010
East of the Mississippi — Jack Lammers 888-461-5007, West of the Mississippi — Jim Secrist 800-976-2298
lammersj@boystown.org
secristj@boystown.org
Help, healing and hope for girls and boys throughout the United States.

Mr. Mike Jorgensen
Executive Vice President
Global Missions Fellowship, Inc.
P. O. Box 742828
Dallas, TX 75374
phone 972-783-7476
fax 972-234-4960
mike.jorgensen@gmf.org
www.gmf.org
To mobilize North American churches to assist local churches in other countries in one-week saturation evangelism/discipleship campaigns with the purpose of establishing new Christian churches in unchurched neighborhoods.

Mr. Wes White
Executive Director
Global Outreach
P. O. Box 1
Tupelo, MS 38802
phone 662-842-4615
fax 662-842-4620
go@globaloutreach.org
Missionary organization.

Mr. John Worley
Director of Development
Gospel Missionary Union
10000 North Oak
Kansas City, MO 64155
phone 816-734-8500
fax 816-734-4601
jworley@gmu.org
www.gmu.org
Evangelical missions-sending agency.

Mr. Stephen Hoffman
Director of Development
Greater Europe Mission
18950 Base Camp Road
Monument, CO 80132
phone 719-488-8008
fax 719-488-8018

Mr. Robert E. Schmidt
CFP, Director of Planned Giving
Habitat for Humanity International
121 Habitat Street
Americus, GA 31709
phone 800-422-4828 ext. 2957
fax 229-928-5464
rschmidt@hfhi.org
www.habitat.org
Partnering with families to build decent, affordable housing.

Mr. John Collins
Administrative Pastor
Harvest Ministries
6115 Arlington Avenue
Riverside, CA 92504
phone 909-687-6902
john@harvest.org
www.harvest.org
To know Christ better and to make Him known.

Mr. Paul Higbee
President
Heal the Nations
4616 West 84th Street
Tulsa, OK 74132
phone 918-446-0185
phigbee@healthenations.com
www.healthenations.com
To improve the health of underdeveloped communities in the world.

Mr. Jerry Kitchel
Vice President, Communications and Advancement
International Aid
17011 West Hickory
Spring Lake, MI 49456
phone 616-846-7490
fax 616-846-3842
kitchelj@internationalaid.org
www.internationalaid.org
Links caring people and organizations with Christian partners worldwide.

Ms. Linda Alumbaugh
Planned Giving Director
International Bible Society
1820 Jet Stream Drive
Colorado Springs, CO 80921-3696
phone 800-448-0456
fax 719-867-2866
pg-jbsf@usa.ibs.org
www.Ibslegacy.org
Translation and distribution of Scriptures.

Mr. Jim Schnabel
Vice President
International Christian Concern
2020 Pennsylvania Avenue NW #941
Washington, DC 20006
phone 301-989-1708
fax 301-989-1709
icc@idsonline.com
www.persecution.com
Works with persecuted Christians.

Dr. Daryl McCarthy
CEO
International Institute for Christian Studies
P. O. Box 12147
Overland Park, KS 66282-2147
phone 913-962-4422
fax 913-962-1912
iics@iics.com
www.iics.com
Placing Christian professors in public universities overseas.

Mr. Robert Lonac
Chief Operating Officer
International Justice Mission
P. O. Box 58147
Washington, DC 20037
phone 703-465-5495
fax 703-465-5499
contact@ijm.org
www.ijm.org
Christian human rights organization.

Rev. Douglas Van Bronkhorst
Executive Director
InterServe/USA
P. O. Box 418
Upper Darby, PA 19082-0418
phone 800-809-4440
fax 610-352-0581
dvb@ludlow.net
www.interserveusa.org
Sending Christian professionals to Asia and the Middle East.

Ms. Diane Riley
Planned Giving Administrator
InterVarsity Christian Fellowship/ USA
P. O. Box 7895
Madison, WI 53707-7895
phone 608-274-9001
fax 608-274-7882
www.ivcf.org
Non-profit parachurch organization (college and university student evangelism).

Mr. Dennis Steenwyck
Administration Department
JAARS, Inc.
P. O. Box 248
Waxhaw, NC 28173-0248
phone 704-843-6288
fax 704-843-6355
www.jaars.org
Providing technical and logistical services for Bible translation.

Joyce Meyer Ministries
700 Grace Parkway
Fenton, MO 63026
phone 800-727-9673
info@joycemeyer.org
www.joycemeyer.org

Kids Alive International
2507 Cumberland Drive
Valpariso, IN 46383
phone 800-543-7330
fax 219-462-5611
kidsalive@kidsalive.org
www.kidsalive.org
Kids Alive International will reflect the love of Christ by rescuing suffering children in crisis, nurturing them with quality holistic care and introducing them to the transforming power of Jesus Christ so they are able to instill hope in others. We remember the call of James 1:27.

Mr. Jose Zirena
Director of Finance
Latin America Mission
P. O. Box 52-7900
Miami, FL 33152-7900
phone 305-884-8400
fax 305-885-8649
jzirena@lam.org
www.lam.org
Working in the Latin church.

Ms. Sharson Gill
CEO
LifeSteps Foundation, Inc.
4888 10th Avenue North
Greenacres, FL 33463
phone 561-967-4066
fax 561-967-4640
sharon.gill@lifesteps.org
www.lifesteps.org
Education missionaries.

Pike Lambedh
Vice President
The Lockman Foundation
900 South Euclid Street
La Habra, CA 90631
phone 714-879-3055
fax 714-879-3058
www.lockman.org
An interdemonimational ministry dedicated to the translation, publication, and distribution of the New American Standard Bible, La Biblia de las Americas, and the Amplified Bible.

Pastor David Jinno
President
Love-N-Care Ministries USA
P. O. Box 535
No. Bennington, VT 05257-0535
phone 802-442-2711
mail@love-n-careministries.org
www.love-n-careministries.org
Ministering to the needs of people through Christian evangelism, children's homes, education and ministry training, old age homes, medical clinics and hospitals, and vocational training, especially in India, USA and Canada.

Mr. Ron Frey
Director of Development Communications
Luis Palau Evangelistic Association
P. O. Box 1173
Portland, OR 97207-1173
phone 503-614-1500
fax 503-614-1599
r_frey@palau.org
www.lpea.org
Proclaim the Gospel, mobilize the church, equip the next generation.

Dr. Wrede Vogel
Executive Director
Luke Society, Inc.
2204 South Minnesota Avenue, Ste. 200
Sioux Falls, SD 57105
phone 605-373-9686
fax 605-373-9711
office@lukesociety.org
www.lukesociety.org
Medical missions

Dr. Marshall R. Gillam
Executive Director
Lutheran Bible Translators
P. O. Box 2050
Aurora, IL 60507-2050
phone 630-897-0660
fax 630-897-3567
info@LBT.org
www.LBT.org
The mission of Lutheran Bible Translators is to help bring people to faith in Jesus Christ by making the Word of God available to those who do not yet have it in the language of their hearts.

Mr. Dwight Jarboe
Director
MMS Aviation
P. O. Box 1118
Coshocton, OH 43812-6118
phone 740-622-6848
fax 740-622-8277
admin@mmsaviation.org
www.mmsaviation.org
To prepare people and airplanes for worldwide mission service.

Rev. Peter Marshall
Peter Marshall Ministries
81 Finlay Road
Orleans, MA 02653
phone 508-255-7705
Revival preaching for churches and teaching on America's Christian heritage.

Mr. Al Menconi
President
Al Menconi Ministries
P. O. Box 131147
Carlsbad, CA 92013
phone 760-591-4696
fax 760-591-4698
info@almenconi.com
www.almenconi.com
To educate parents about entertainment and media so they can, in turn, teach their kids about values.

Mr. James Schaffer
Director of Development
Ministries Study Center
490 Prospect Street
New Haven, CT 06511
phone 203-624-6672
fax 203-865-2857
schaffer@omsc.org
www.omsc.org
Residential programs for the renewal of missionaries and overseas church leaders and the advancement of mission research and publication.

Dr. John F. McGeorge, President
Ministry to Eastern Europe
2520 Professional Road, Ste. C
Richmond, VA 23235
phone 804-320-6456
fax 804-320-6456
mtee@erols.com
www.gospelcom.net/mtee
To train a new generation of spiritual leaders throughout Eastern Europe.

Mr. LaVand (Van) Syverson
President
Mission Aviation Fellowship
P. O. Box 3202
Redlands, CA 92373
phone 909-794-1151
fax 909-794-3016
Vsyverson@maf.org
www.maf.org
To multiply the effectiveness of the church using aviation and other strategic technologies to conquer barriers in reaching the world for Christ.

Mr. Bob Losch
Mission Possible
1587 Broadview Drive
Jenison, MI 49428
phone 616-457-3564
fax 616-457-2145
missionpossible@cs.com
www.missionpossible.org
To impact young people and adults so that missions become a vital part of their lives and to offer opportunities to affect the world for Christ.

Dr. Rob Helmer
President
Missionair, Inc.
150 South Roma Way
Kissimmee, FL 34746
phone 407-397-1109
fax 407-397-1913
missions@missionair.org
www.missionair.org
Short-term mission trips, missionary support, disaster relief.

Mr. Paul Fleischmann
CEO
National Network of Youth Ministries
12335 World Trade Drive, Ste. 16
San Diego, CA 92128
phone 858-451-1111
fax 858-451-6900
paulf@nnym.org
www.youthworkers.net
Youth ministry cooperation/networking.

Mr. Bill Moritz
Estate and Financial Planning
The Navigators
P. O. Box 6000
Colorado Springs, CO 80934
phone 719-594-2427
fax 719-266-4604
vwmoritz@aol.com
www.navigators.org
Discipleship and evangelism.

Ms. Diane Lostrangio
ExecutiveDirector
New Hope Child & Family Agency
19304 King's Garden Drive North
Seattle, WA 98133
phone 206-363-1800
fax 206-363-0318
info@newhopekids.org
www.newhope4adoption.org
Adoption agency – New Hope works actively and compassionately to extend the love of Christ to those we serve.

Ms. Soozi Redkey
Vice President Development
Northwest Medical Teams International
P. O. Box 10
Portland, OR 97207-0010
phone 503-624-1000
fax 503-624-1001
sredkey@nwmti.org
www.nwmti.org
International relief/humanitarian aid.

Mr. Harry Halkowich
Stewardship Ministries Director
OMF International
10 West Dry Creek Circle
Littleton, CO 80120-4413
phone 800-422-5330
fax 303-730-4165
hhalkowich@omf.org
www.us.omf.org
Our mission is to glorify God by the urgent evangelization of East Asia's peoples.

Mr. Richard John
Vice President of Finance
Opportunity International
2122 York Road, Ste. 340
Oak Brook, IL 60523
phone 630-645-4100
Micro economic development (MED).

Mr. Mark Sigmon
Executive Director
Outreach, Inc.
3140 Three Mile Road NE
Grand Rapids, MI 49525-3165
phone 616-363-7817
fax 616-363-7880
info@outreachmission.org
www.outreachmission.org
Equipping global leaders for local churches through leadership training.

Mr. Jerry Wall
Advancement Administrator
Peacemaker Ministries
1537 Avenue D, Suite 352
Billings, MT 59102
phone 406-256-1583
fax 406-256-0001
mail@hispeace.org
www.hispeace.org
Biblical conflict resolution.

Mr. John W. Davidson
Asst. to the President
Pioneers USA
12343 Narcoossee Road
Orlando, FL 32827
phone 407-382-6000
jwdchapin@yahoo.com
www.pioneers.org
Evangelization and church planting among unreached peoples.

Pastor Ed Nesselhuf
Director
Prison Congregations of America
P. O. Box 415
Vermillion, SD 57069-0415
phone 605-624-8330
fax 605-624-3123
pastored@iw.net
www.prisoncongregations.org
Develop Christian congregations within state prisons in the United States.

Mr. Joe Patak
National Ministry Director
Project Partner with Christ, Inc.
P. O. Box 610
Springboro, OH 45066
phone 513-425-0938
fax 513-425-6628
partner@projectpartner.com
Train and equip indigenous national leaders.

Mr. Jeffrey B. Wilson
Director of Major Gifts
Promise Keepers
P. O. Box 103001
Denver, CO 80250-3001
phone 303-964-7600
fax 303-964-7926
finance@pknet.org
www.promisekeepers.org
Christ-centered ministry dedicated to uniting men through vital relationships to become godly influences in their world.

Mr. Max E. Smith
RBC Ministries
P. O. Box 2222
Grand Rapids, MI 49555-0001
phone 616-974-2701
fax 616-957-5741
msmith@rbc.org
www.gospelcom.net/rbc
Lead people to faith in Christ and growth in Christlikeness.

Mr. Michael Dey
Stewardship Department
SIM USA, Inc.
P. O. Box 7900
Charlotte, NC 28241
phone 704-588-4300
fax 704-587-1518
stewardship@sim.org
www.sim.org
SIM exists to glorify God by planting, strengthening and partnering with churches around the world as we evangelize the unreached, minister to human need, disciple believers into churches, and equip churches to fulfill Christ's commission.

Mr. Frank Moselely
Co-Founder
SOS International
5201 Roe Blvd.
Roeland Park, KS 66205
phone 913-432-2SOS (2767)
fax 913-384-3777
fwm@soshelp.com
www.soshelp.com
A spiritual lifeline focused on the one act (Salvation) that touches all eternity.

Major George Hood
National Community Relations - Development Secretary
Salvation Army
615 Slaters Lane
Alexandria, VA 22314
phone 703-684-5500
fax 703-684-5538
george_hood@usn.salvationarmy.org

Mr. Harry Van Burik
International Program Director
Shelter For Life
P. O. Box 1306
Oshkosh, WI 54903
phone 920-426-1207
fax 920-426-4321
harry@shelter.org
www.shelter.org
Non-profit Christian relief and development.

Mr. Raymond Walker
Chief Financial Officer
Source of Light Ministries
1011 Mission Road
Madison, GA 30650
phone 706-342-0397
fax 706-342-9072
solm@sourcelight.org
www.sourcelight.org
Bible correspondence course, Christian printing.

Mr. Ray A. Buchanan
President & CEO
Stop Hunger Now
2501 ClarkAvenue, Ste. 301
Raleigh, NC 27607-7213
phone 888-501-8440
fax 919-839-8971
info@stophungernow.org
www.stophungernow.org
Emergency and disaster response, food and medicine.

Rev. John Castellani
Teen Challenge International
P. O. Box 1015
Springfield, MO 65801
phone 417-862-6969
fax 417-862-8209
tcusa@teenchallengeusa.com
www.teenchallenge.com
Faith-based drug and alcohol rehabilitation and discipleship.

Mr. Tim Klingbeil
Chief Development Officer
Trans World Radio
P. O. Box 8700
Cary, NC 27512
phone 800-456-7TWR
fax 919-460-3702
info@twr.org
www.twr.org
Broadcasting the Gospel in over 180 languages around the world.

Mr. Bob Butts
Executive Director
Truth for Life
P.O. Box 398000
Cleveland, OH 44139
phone 440-708-2119
fax 440-543-0522
bob@truthforlife.org
www.truthforlife.org
The Bible teaching ministry of Alistair Begg. The program is distributed via radio and internet.

United Prayer Tower
801 Front avenue
St. Paul, MN 55103
phone 651-487-5827
fax 651-487-5936
unitedpt@aol.com

Mr. Kevin Shantz
Business Manager
Uplook Ministries
P. O. Box 2041
Grand Rapids, MI 49501-2041
phone 616-456-9166
fax 616-456-5522
kevin@uplook.org
www.uplook.org
Christian publishing.

Mr. Ken Briden
Operations Director
VELA Ministries International
P. O. Box 28840
San Jose, CA 95159
phone 408-995-5090
fax 408-995-5092
vela-sj@velaministries.org
www.velaministries.org
Latin American missions organization.

Ms. Barbara Lamb Hall
Director of Development
Village Enterprise Fund
751 Laurel Street, #222
San Carlos, CA 94070
phone 650-802-8891
fax 650-802-8890
vefmail@aol.com
www.villageef.org
Microbusiness seed capital and training in development countries.

Dr. Phil Corson
Development
Westwood Ministries
P. O. Box 291446
Kerrville, TX 78029
phone 800-583-9841
fax 830-634-7001
westwood@ktc.com
www.westwoodministries.org
An interdenominational ministry dedicated to the health and healing of Christian leaders and their families. Ministries offered include counseling, mentoring, sabbatical/retreat, life/ministry training and church counseling.

Milan Anderson, Vice President
World Harvest Now
P. O. Box 911
Denton, TX 76202
phone 940-891-4400
fax 940-484-6097
whn@whn.org
www.whn.org
Missions.

Ms. Jo Anne Lyon, Executive Director
World Hope International, Inc.
8136 Old Keene Mill Rd., Ste. 209A
Springfield, VA 22152
phone 888-466-4673
joanne@worldhope.net
www.worldhope.net

Mr. Don Allsman, VP Strategic Planning
World Impact
2001 South Vermont Avenue
Los Angeles, CA 90007
phone 323-735-1137
fax 323-735-2576
dallsman@worldimpact.org
www.worldimpact.org
Inner-city missions.

Mr. Scott Vander Kooy
President
Worldwide Christian Schools
1009 44th Street, Ste. B
Grand Rapids, MI 49509-4177
phone 616-531-9102
fax 616-531-0602
svanderkooy@wwcs.org
www.wwcs.org
Development of Christian schools mainly in third-world countries.

Mr. Jeff Rudder
Director of Gift Planning
Young Life
P. O. Box 520
Colorado Springs, CO 80901
phone 719-381-1887
fax 719-381-1755
giftplan@sc.younglife.org
www.younglife.org
Youth evangelism.

For the most complete and up-to-date listings, please visit our website:
www.christianestateplanners.org

"When you cease to make a contribution, you begin to die."

Eleanor Roosevelt

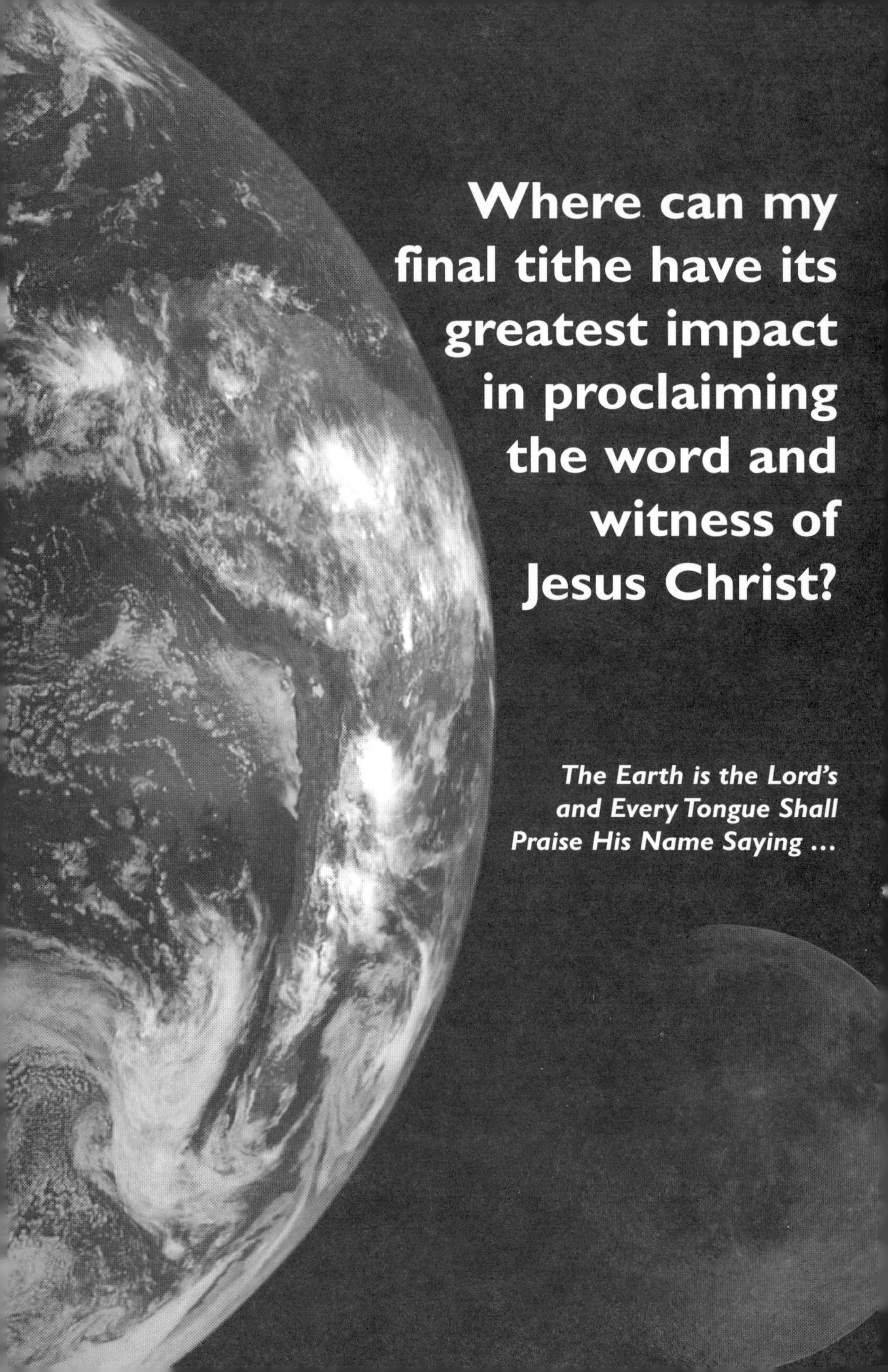

Where can my final tithe have its greatest impact in proclaiming the word and witness of Jesus Christ?

The Earth is the Lord's and Every Tongue Shall Praise His Name Saying …

Onde pode ter o meu dizimo final o seu impacto mais grande em proclamar a palavra e a testemunha de Jesús Cristo?

Wo kann mein letzter Zehnt den grössten Eindruck machen auf die Verkündung des Wortes und Zeugnis von Jesus Christus?

Hol gyakorolhatná végső tizedem a legnagyobb hatást Jézus Krisztus tanainak hirdetésére?

Ubi mea ultima decuma habēre potest maximum ictum pronuntians Verbum Arbitremque Jesus Christi?

Où ma dernière dîme peut-elle faire avancer le plus efficacement l'annonciation de la parole et du témoignage de Jésus-Christ?

Kvar kan den siste tienda mi få størst mogleg nerknad i det å forkynne Jesu Kristi ord og vitnebyrd?

¿Dónde puede tener mi último diezmo su mayor influencia en proclamar la palabra y el testimonio de Jesus Cristo?

Hvor kan min sidste tiendedel få sin største virksomhed i proklamationen af ordet til og vidnesbyrdet om Jesus Christus?

Nae hun gum yee Ye su Geu ree seu do ae mal goa jeung kuh rul nah tah nae nun deh yeet suh suh Uh dee eh kah jang kun young hyang eul joo nun kah?

www.christianestateplanners.or

FELLOWSHIP OF CHRISTIAN ESTATE PLANNERS

"Haven't you read this scripture: " 'The stone the builders rejected has become the capstone; the Lord has done this, and it is marvelous in our eyes' ?"
— Mark 12:10-11

CHAPTER 16

With nearly $20 trillion in projected estate transfers during the next 20 years and only six percent of active church members currently providing for their churches and Christian-related organizations in their estates, the Fellowship of Christian Estate Planners, Inc., a non-profit corporation, was founded for the purpose of promoting biblically based estate planning.

The goal is to make all Christians aware of the biblical principles of stewardship in not only their daily lives but also their estate planning.

The Board of Directors grants associate membership to any person who agrees to provide a Christian witness of stewardship in their professional work and utilize the general principles of Christian estate planning.

The foundation is supported by a free-will offering from affiliated members, foundation grants and other gifts. It does not have paid membership.

A Website (www.christianestateplanners.org) is the common gathering place of information, ideas and innovation in Christian estate planning to support affiliated members. It also provides links to other compatible Christian resource sites to maximize the information available for Christian estate planning.

While not limited by profession, the Fellowship of Christian Estate Planners invites Christian attorneys, trust officers, life insurance agents, development directors, brokers, financial planners and similar professionals as affiliated members.

This non-profit corporation was founded by Rollyn H. Samp, author of *The Final Tithe: A Christian Approach to Estate Planning*. It is governed by a five-person independent Board of Directors who manage the foundation.

FELLOWSHIP OF CHRISTIAN ESTATE PLANNERS MISSION

To energize committed Christian professionals working in Estate Planning to present the Final Tithe as a daily witness to their family, associates, friends and clients.

BOARD OF DIRECTORS

RICHARD GORSUCH

Mr. Gorsuch is one of America's most talented Christian visual communicators. His graphic work "Heavy Thinking" and evangelism media resources have been used by hundreds of churches throughout the country. Creating visual "marketplace friendly" ministry concepts with ideas based on solid theology, Richard's innovative print images communicate the love of the Lord and present the reality of the Good News in a way that attracts many to Jesus Christ.

CHAPLAIN JOHN LUNDIN

Colonel Lundin has had a distinguished career as a pastor and military chaplain. Recently retired as chaplain at Andrews Air Force Base, he has developed extensive family service and religious programs for armed services families and has served worldwide in a variety of pastoral positions.

PAUL RIDGEWAY

Mr. Ridgeway is one of the world's leading special event creators with involvement in numerous Super Bowls, Washington for Jesus, Hands Across America, Pope Paul's USA visit, and other related mega-events. He is also an active Christian layman who is a frequent speaker on witnessing.

ROLLYN SAMP

Mr. Samp has served as Chief of Staff for the Governor of South Dakota, Field Representative to the first Native American elected to Congress, and Chief Tribal Court Judge. He has been president of his church and involved on numerous boards, as well as working on special church projects. After 30 years of practicing law, he founded the Fellowship of Christian Estate Planners. He is the author of *If You Liked the '50s, You'll Love These Stories* and *The Final Tithe: A Christian Approach to Estate Planning*, along with a weekly newspaper column called "What's the Law?" with over 400,000 readers. He can be reached via E-mail at rsamp@samplaw.com.

REVEREND AL VERBURG

The holder of two divinity degrees and presently working on a doctorate in psychology, Mr. VerBurg is one of the leading Christian counselors in America whose unique approach to solving people problems brings an important balance of theological background and practical family problem-solving to the Board.

POSTWORD

Meet The Author

Rolly Samp is an attorney with multiple business and professional interests including law, lobbying, writing, lecturing, politics and communications.

He holds a degree in political science and communications from Augustana College and a Juris Doctorate from the University of South Dakota.

While at Augustana, Samp was a member of their national-champion college debate team. He was selected for the Sen. Francis Case Leadership Award and Sen. Robert Taft Award, among other honors. He and his wife, Karen, were the *Argus Leader* newlywed "Couple of the Year" in 1964.

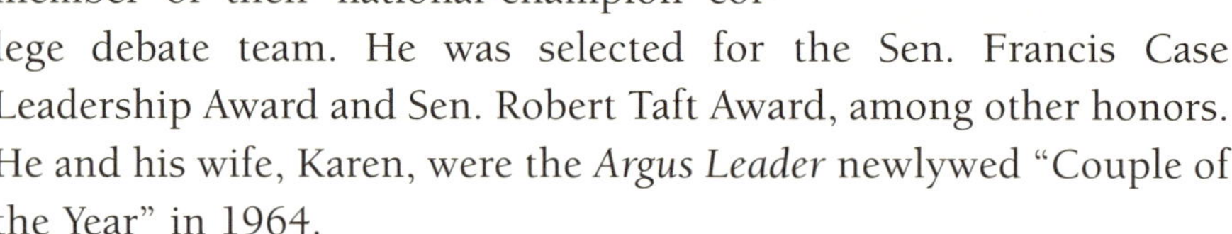

Samp served for five-and-a-half years heading the South Dakota field staff of U. S. Representative Ben Reifel, the first Plains Native American elected to the United States Congress.

At age 25, he became Chief of Staff to the Governor of South Dakota. He began his private legal practice in 1971.

He is credited with authoring the state's economic development incentive tax laws, administrative procedural law, and the rural ambulance program, together with local option tax legislation.

Among his many civic activities, Samp in 1972-1973 organized a citizen group to successfully authorize and fund a four-year medical school for the state. In 1976, he helped lead the statewide fight for repeal of a dairy marketing law which had artificially fixed milk prices. He successfully fought for authorization of private college student funding in 1976. In 1977, Samp was one of the leaders who worked to remove a 40-year ban on championship high school football playoffs in the state.

In 1998, he served on the Governor's Task Force on Trust Reform which led efforts to successfully revise the State's surety and trust laws. He co-authored a South Dakota Law Review article on trusts in 1999.

Rolly Samp served eight years as Chief Tribal Judge of the Flandreau Santee Sioux Tribe. He has been active in Native American law including his work with Honorable Ben Reifel as Congressman and former Commissioner of the Bureau of Indian Affairs. He was involved in successfully defeating a state referendum which would have allowed state jurisdiction over Indian reservations. He assisted in organizing the United Sioux Tribes, Inc. Rolly and Karen have helped raise several Native American foster children.

In 1986, the United Sioux Tribes gave him their highest honor with a blessed peace pipe as thanks for over three decades of service to Native Americans. He was a member of the Northern Plains Tribal Judges Association.

In 1985, he was a founder of "Save Our Lakes" and served as President from 1987 to 1991.

For many years, Samp was President of the Dakota Chapter, Cystic Fibrosis Foundation and founder of the Cystic Fibrosis Clinics of the state. He was chairman of the Minnehaha County Ambulance Study in 1993.

He helped author and coordinated the publication of a book entitled *Governors of South Dakota*. His weekly "What's the Law?" newspaper column has approximately 400,000 readers. He has appeared in several national publications including *Communicating for Agriculture, Farm Journal, Outdoor Life,* and *Conservation Digest.* He was a consultant for the Dan Rather-CBS News South Dakota "farm crisis" week-long television special in 1987.

Rolly was a volunteer YMCA youth basketball coach for 18

years, spent over five years as a Boy Scout leader, a member of the local library board, and has held numerous church, civic and charitable positions. In 1989, he was recipient of the Friend of 4-H award and received the Humanitarian of the Year award in 1990.

He served as Vice-President and President of Hope Lutheran Church and several years as a delegate to the Augustana College Association, the Crossroads Conference, and the South Dakota ELCA Synod Committee. He also served on the Augustana College Fellow Cabinet. Samp is the founder of the Fellowship of Christian Estate Planners.

He is the author of *If You Liked the '50s, You'll Love These Stories.*

Rolly and Karen Samp have four children, Michael, Matthew, Rebecca and Elizabeth, in addition to serving as foster parents to nearly 70 youth.

About the Design

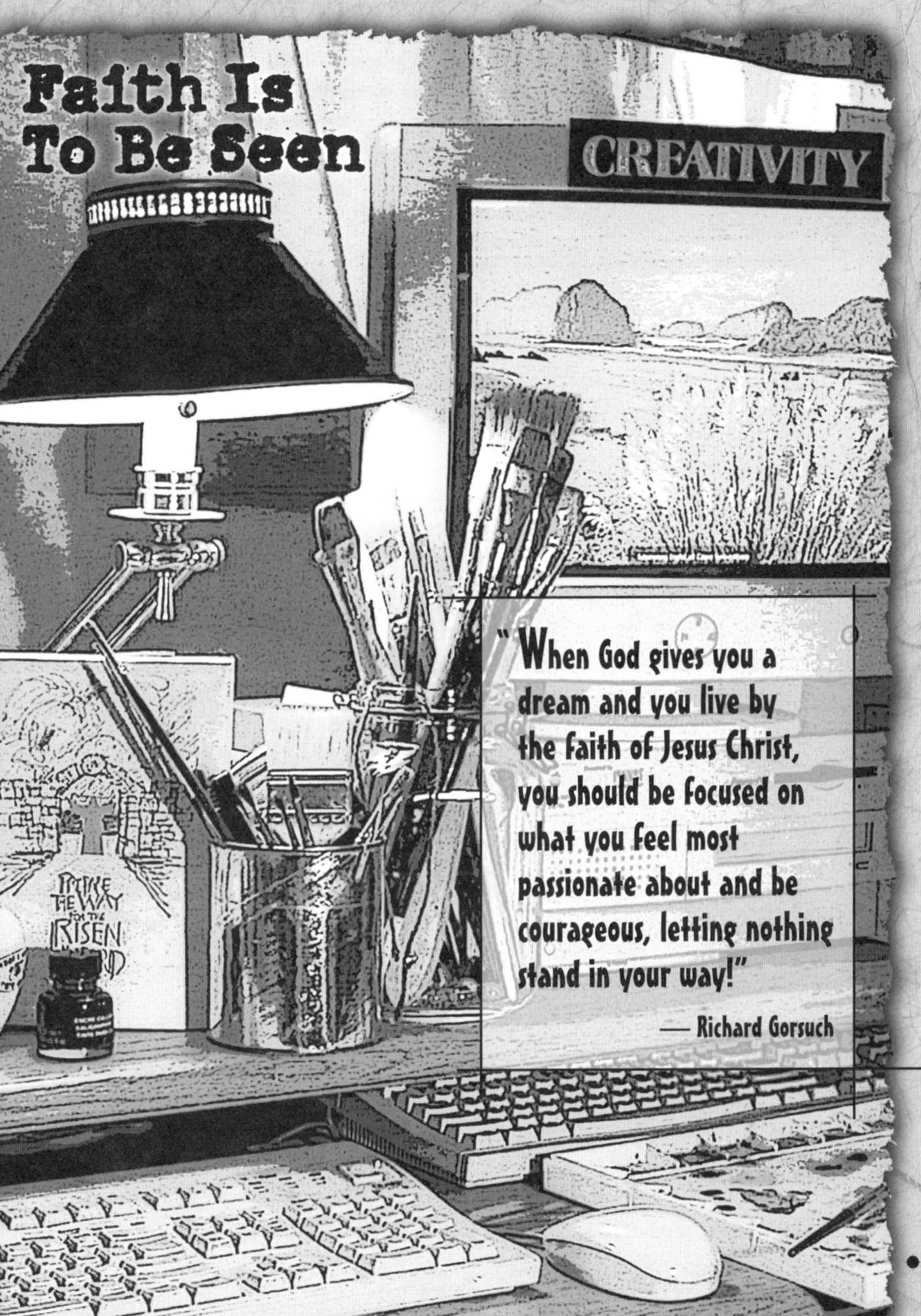

Meet Richard Gorsuch

Richard Gorsuch was called by God to a lifelong work of visually communicating Christ. The call didn't come via telephone. He didn't get a wake up call by a bolt of lightning. But the call came in a near death experience at the Mayo Clinic in 1965. Gorsuch began his communication career marketing ice cream and candy bars. But he found in his conversion experiences from a Gideon Bible something even sweeter to market – the Gospel of Jesus Christ. A car accident had landed him in the prestigious hospital. While the accident injuries were not life-threatening, a tumor was discovered that could have been.

"As I gave my life to Christ in that hospital room and my life was handed back to me, I knew God had a plan for my work," Gorsuch recounts. "He didn't promise me a smooth walk but a clear path to eternity."

Gorsuch thought of becoming a pastor but realized his talents were in art. Deep into the scriptures and prayer over the years, God has led his pen and now Pentium driven computer to move the hearts of people toward Christ.

Well qualified for God's calling with a University Degree in Art and Art Studies at the University of Mexico, Gorsuch initially found a lonely world, both professionally and within many churches who were reluctant to fund innovative evangelical ideas. But he never succumbed to these market constraints. God led him to projects where he could match the promise of Christ with the visual message of each work. His "Heavy Thinking" Christian newspaper visual message found its way into over 500 newspapers. Christian health care, schools and retirement organizations sought him to plant Christ's message into their marketing. And while national awards resulted, the personal rewards of spiritual growth flowed as he humbly asked God each day, "What am I to do for you today?"

"Many artists go for the eye, I go for the heart."

– Richard Gorsuch

SUCCESS IN COMMUNICATING CHRIST

After teaming up with writer Rolly Samp in the 1970s for an award winning massive multi-media project successfully authorizing a four year medical school for South Dakota and other projects, the two traveled separate professional paths, yet always staying in touch on a personal and spiritual level.

The odd couple; A lawyer/writer and an artist with a unique understanding of what they could accomplish working together on a Christian work for the marketplace.

Samp overrode publishers and doubters in his demand that "The Final Tithe" be illustrated by Richard Gorsuch. "This is one of the toughest subjects within the church and people's lives. Only Gorsuch can visually bring alive the joy of giving," Samp would tell associates. "He's the best. There's no second place for God's work."

So the two began merging the words with visual concepts in a way never done before in a book about law, life and giving. It took over two years to weave the right graphic concept throughout the book. "But it was worth the wait," Samp says. "God created everything in six days. We work a little slower."

WHAT IS A CHRISTIAN VISUAL COMMUNICATOR?

No one ever asked that question of Michelangelo, a Gorsuch hero, who defied conventional wisdom to create everlasting images of Christ via an image on a church ceiling and in dozens of other mediums. But it is an important question.

In a contemporary sense, many Christians will recall Gorsuch's national efforts with the media campaign, "I love you. Is that O.K.? – J. Christ" and "In Christ's Love, Everyone is Someone" visual communications of Christ to the masses.

Those are just a couple of glitzy high-profile examples of his work. But what does Gorsuch do? Richard Gorsuch has been answering that question for over four decades. But it is his work that really tells the story. How he works is something he eagerly shares with all who will listen, in hopes of inspiring others. It is a daily witness for those who cross his path.

GORSUCH'S SIX STEPS TO VISUALLY SHARING CHRIST'S PROMISE...

The Image

"Whatever is created comes from the Word. God inspires if you seek the Word and listen to his voice while tuning out the world."

The Concept

"When God gives you the image, it needs to stick like a postage stamp. I create the stamp and stick it on the message trusting God to deliver it."

Seeing is Believing

"You've heard the old expression, 'A picture is worth a thousand words,' – there's an even better description in a Chinese proverb,

'That which enters the eye, will never leave the heart.' Many artists go for the eye, I go for the heart."

Seed Faith

"When you visually reach someone's heart for Christ, you plant a seed. If the seed is cultivated, weeds pulled and, if it is watered and well tended, it will continue to grow, blossom and share its beauty. That's the life of a Believer. You never get the complete beauty and aroma of the flower until a Christian goes through these steps in their faith walk."

Why Christian Art?

"Because most people are visual communicators. The world has conditioned us to make decisions on images like eating under the Golden Arches to 'dot com' campaigns driving our curiosity. The seed of Christ can be planted just as quickly as a few second television commercial. But it takes a lifetime to fully grow the commitment. Christian visual communications are a key to unlocking the door of God's promises to a hungry world searching for meaning. The soul is thirsty for Truth and reality."

Invitation, Not Invasion

"Christian communications should be an invitation to Christ, not an invasion into lives which might turn people away from the Cross. Communicating the unknown requires use of the known. Earth, water, sun, sky, trees, people, the Word – all of God's creation is an invitation to come close to Christ."

TODAY AND BEYOND...

Today, like every day, Richard Gorsuch begins before sunrise in prayer and meditation by the sea in a 21st Century studio. "Get up, keep up and keep going" are his guideposts. Then he begins his daily work honing the gardens of God's people through his unique visual communication skills. With his wife Bonny and two boys Colour and Sketch, they find life by the sea on the Oregon coast a mixture of inspiration and intimacy with God's creation.

"Most of the book of Genesis is here. And I believe God wants me to use what he first created to visually help people find their way to the cross," Gorsuch adds. "The Final Tithe is not about money. I wouldn't do a book about money. It is a 21st Century call to Christians to celebrate the Joy of Giving. And as we are saved, we need God's help in learning how to give. Rolly Samp put words on paper. I created images to plant the words in the hearts of readers. But God had his hand on both of us as He will you if you simply ask, 'What am I supposed to be doing today?'"

"Great things sprout from a handful of tiny seeds — each bearing dreams of hope."

— Richard Gorsuch

Meet Neil Isaacson

Neil Isaacson, digital designer and consultant extraordinaire, is a collaborator and essential creative comrade with mentor, Richard Gorsuch. Together, they blend their differing abilities and artistic skills to render the graphic image messages seen in The Final Tithe.

As a bass player, Neil feels there is a mystical creative relationship between making music and co-creating graphic images with another artist. In performance with an ensemble, or laying down tracks in a recording studio, a musician learns to share in the creative exchange of ideas. The images between Neil and Richard are an improvisation in visual composition.

When Neil touches the keyboard of his Macintosh his fingers make a similar kind of music that has been part of his career as a professional musician. The nightclub music gigs of his past gradually evolved into playing tunes that carried a wholesome message and entertained people in concerts, churches and festivals.

"It's a fun way to live my life," he said. "I can arrange tunes, relate to an audience and play music in worship settings. Plus my work as a designer allows me to sit at my Mac and create digital illustrations and design layouts reflecting the mood and message of a Christian manuscript that appeals to the eye."

Leaving his Midwest roots, Neil, his wife, and family found what they were missing in life in Oregon, where God uses his talents doing the layout and design on Christian books and similar projects.

"A graphic design can change or enhance the mood of a writing just like a song can alter the feelings of an audience," Isaacson relates. "I love lifting up people for Christ whether making a book reader-friendly or in a music setting offering new experiences to those seeking something more from life."

"The Final Tithe gave me a chance to use talents God gave me; some I didn't even know I had."

Neil has developed a special synergy working with Richard Gorsuch. He says, "It begins with the Word and ends in our Work."

SPECIAL ACKNOWLEDGMENT

Thank you to these committed Christians who gave their time, ideas and encouragement to the success of this publication:

Mel Anderson
Reverends Michael and Vicki Bang
Kent Boadwine
Duayne and Cyndy Boesch
Pat Boone
Todd and Kim Brua
Dr. George K. Brushaber
Bishop Robert J. Carlson
Les Carson
Pat Correa
Dale Dawson
Monsignor James Doyle
Bishop Norm Eitreim
Ralna English
Chris Eng
David Fermenich
Reverend Roger Fredrickson
Jon Haller
Gary and Randi Helder
Stacey Hennen
Gerry and Monica Heuer
John Hoffman
Reverend Dr. Roald Kindem
Sister Janice Klein
Gary Kulm
Rick Lingberg
Col. John Lundin (ret)
Pastor Jerry Merkouris
Margaret Mesmer
James P. Moore
Jon Mostrom
Professor Mike Myers
Reverend Jim and Ruth Mullen
Tom and Martha Nelson
Dr. William C. Nelsen
Dave Olson
Reverend Dr. Val Putnam
Dr. Paul A. Rader
Paul Ridgeway
Ardyce Samp
Elizabeth Samp
Matthew Samp
Michael and Julie Samp
Julie Smith
Ralph Stewart
Vi Stoia
Gerald Teunissen
Reverend Ron Traub
Reverend Dr. Al VerBurg
Eric and Rebecca Vostad
Reverend Paul Votaw
Sheila Wright
Paul Wentzlaff

www.christianestateplanners.org

Father Goes To Holy Land

Father James O'Brian is getting a dream trip thanks to the will of one of his parishioners, Russell Dougherty, who passed away last month.

A longtime member of the Holy Mary Catholic Church, Dougherty specified in his will that Father O'Brian would get an all expense paid trip to the Holy Land, Rome, and Greece and be able to select another person to go with him.

Father O'Brian said he was "shocked" by the gift. "Mr. Dougherty always said when he passed away I'd be the happiest person in church, but he was kind of a jokester. I thought he was just making conversation."

Father O'Brian plans to spend extra time during the trip visiting the Vatican and early Christian sites in Greece.

"This is something you only dream about and be thankful Mr. Dougherty found such a special way to remember someone in his will."

Scholarship For Seminary Students

A Quad City couple has made sure students entering the ministry have adequate funds for their seminary expenses. The wills of Samuel and Manetta Baker left a gift of $250,000 in the Central Baptist Church fund to be used for seminary students.

The couple, who died within the last two years, had belonged to the church for over 45 years. They left 25% of their estate for support of seminary students, with the balance to several nieces and nephews.

"They believed we needed to recruit more clergy and wanted to do their part to see this financially happen," said Ennis Baker, administrator of the estate. "They put the church first and that's been a great lesson for all of the family."

Estate Gift Helps Missionaries

Jack Parker never traveled to Africa. But in his will he remembered the people of Africa with a special gift to the Christian Outreach Mission in Africa.

"He had a real commitment to missions, giving to them during his lifetime, writing missionaries and encouraging them and taking part in many special events on missions," his wife Mildred Parker said. "And in his will he made sure the first 10% went into a fund to help with these missions. He always said the family would be happy with what ever they got and he wanted to support the mission program after he was gone."

Mrs. Parker said the day he made his will and told her what he was going to do "was one of the happiest days of his life. It was like he had a new purpose."

...ficials
...equest w
...he fund
... the c
...ical cor
...allow
...com
...in
...n.

ESTATE NEWS —

New Church Carpet

A Watertown lady, who neighbors described as a frugal church go... recluse, gave her church something in her will she never had — new carp...

Maude Everling worked as a cook until retirement. She atten... Downtown Methodist Church every Sunday. "She was always quiet ab... her giving," her son said when he relayed to the family that Mrs. Ever... had saved $11,500 for new church carpet and put in her will that it should... paid first before distributing the rest of her estate.

The church plans to place a plaque on the wall remembering the g... according to church sources, "she's an inspiration in giving to us all."

Estate Endows Daycare Center

Ruth Montgomery never lost her desire to support younger members of her church. Passing away at age 98 late last year, Mrs. Montgomery left $500,000 of her estate to remodel and endow a daycare within the church.

"She specifically requested the endowment be used to support lower income parents on a sliding scale, so their children could have first class Christian daycare," the executor of her estate reported.

Mrs. Montgomery left 30% of her estate for the church and the rest to her three children.

"She made a major faith statement in her will which will be something we can use to help families in a way we have never been able to do before," the church president said in accepting the gift.

Will Finances New Dorm

A new dorm will be built on the campus of Christian College thanks to the estate of William and Martha Sauckwest. The couple had met while students at the college in 1942.

A successful real estate developer, Sauckwest left $10 million for a new dorm to be built on campus.

In their will, the couple left a statement of faith they asked be placed on a bronzed plaque in the entrances entitled "Learners and Givers."

College officials say they are thrilled the couple remembered the college in their will.